Epitaphs of Bomber Command

Epitaphs of Bomber Command
By
Steve Darlow and Dave Gilbert

Published in 2025 by Fighting High Ltd
www.fightinghigh.com

Copyright © Fighting High Ltd, 2025
Copyright text © Steve Darlow, 2025
Copyright text © David Gilbert, 2025

The rights of Steve Darlow and David Gilbert to be identified as the authors of this book are asserted in accordance with the Copyright, Patents and Designs Act 1988.

The print publication is protected by copyright. Prior to any prohibited reproduction, storage in a retrieval system, distribution or transmission in any form or by any means, electronic, mechanical, recording or otherwise, permission should be obtained from the publisher.

The ePublication is protected by copyright and must not be copied, reproduced, transferred, distributed, leased, licensed or publicly performed or used in any way except as specifically permitted in writing by the publisher, as allowed under the terms and conditions under which it was purchased, or as strictly permitted by applicable copyright law. Any unauthorised distribution or use of this text may be a direct infringement of the authors' and the publisher's rights and those responsible may be liable in law accordingly.

British Library Cataloguing-in-Publication data. A CIP record for this title is available from the British Library.

ISBN – 13: 978-1-8380687-7-6

Designed by Fighting High.

Printed and bound in Wales by Gomer Press.
Front cover design by Michael Lindley.

Dedication

*To my late parents, Pete and Sheila.
I came into this world with nothing but good parents.
As it turned out, that was all that was necessary.*
(Dave Gilbert)

*To my grandmother Anna, who received the news that
her husband was missing, twice.*
(Steve Darlow)

Berlin 1939 - 1945 War Cemetery

Contents

Author Note	viii
Introduction by Dave Gilbert	ix
Introduction by Steve Darlow	xiii
The Epitaphs	1
Endnotes	111
Acknowledgements	116
Glossary	117
Index	119

Author Note

When examining the epitaphs the authors present their personal interpretations of the feelings behind the choices. Unable to speak directly to the respective relatives, these are, of course, opinions, subject to conjecture. The authors make no claim that their interpretations are definitive and invite the reader to interpret and draw their own conclusions. The epitaphs featured at the beginning of each entry in this book are also quoted verbatim. The authors felt the epitaphs should read exactly as they appear on the respective headstones and any punctuation or grammar suggestions, to assist with interpretation, are therefore highlighted in the main body of the entry.

Introduction

By Dave Gilbert

Epitaphs are of course for the living, not the dead. They offer those who write them some comfort; and those who read them, insight into a life now at its conclusion. Quite literally set in stone, they are perpetual, and as such may address a reader days after the death of the individual or hundreds of years into the future. Long after the records are lost, or the family bible in which their names were written has crumbled, their epitaph remains as the one short touchpoint that endures long into the future.

Far from simply being a farewell, epitaphs are windows into a story of humanity, conveying the essence of the deceased, hopes and aspirations for the future, but most of all, love. Never more was that true than in the case of epitaphs to those who fell in war, and those of Bomber Command are no exception. With an average age of just twenty-three, there was much for their loved ones to lament, and to question.

I began including epitaphs in the International Bomber Command Centre (IBCC) Losses Database several years after I first made the resource available online. The beauty of a database over a conventional roll of honour, of course, is that it is a living publication that can be expanded over time in all manner of different directions. Once established, a database of its kind can garner much of its content by crowd sourcing, allowing photographs and biographical information to be readily added by family members and researchers alike. And because of the way in which it has been funded, in part by the National Lottery Heritage Fund and in part by the incredible generosity of the people of Lincolnshire and beyond, it is widely understood that it is and will always remain a free-of-charge resource for all, forever.

It is equally important to understand that IBCC stands for the people of Bomber Command and not the machines. It exists to tell the human story in all its many facets. Knowing that Sergeant Charles George Williams RAF of No. 144 Squadron was killed just a few days into the war in a disastrous attack on shipping over Heligoland Bight is one thing. Knowing that he was a mere nineteen years of age and his next of kin were his parents, Charles and Evelyn of Westbury-on-Trym, Gloucestershire begins to add the humanity, not to mention the tragedy. But learning that they chose his epitaph WHEN DUTY WHISPERS LOW, THOU MUST, THE YOUTH REPLIES, I CAN adds a depth to the story of Charles' short life that simply can't be achieved any other way.

I was inspired to add epitaphs to the Losses Database by the chance sighting of a single gravestone inscription: that of Sergeant William McDonald of No. 50 Squadron, who was tragically killed by machine gun fire from the ground on 25th October 1942, when his Avro Lancaster was flying at treetop height to avoid flak during an attack on Milan. The remainder of the crew were mercifully uninjured and were able to nurse their damaged aircraft back to England, where Bill sadly died in hospital a few hours later. It reads: MOTHER, I'VE WEIGHED THE RISKS WHICH I PREFER TO LIVING IN A WORLD DOMINATED BY NAZIS. BILL. I was deeply moved by reading it and, in that moment, I realised what a wonderfully rich addition they would be, and that including them all was as obvious as it was urgent.

Of the 58,000 plus Bomber Command losses included in the database, almost 30,000 have an inscription of some kind. Gathering them together was always going to be a huge task and I originally intended to crowd source them over a winter period as a 'dark nights' project, by putting a call out for volunteers on a local radio station; already a tried and tested technique where IBCC and BBC Radio Lincolnshire are concerned.

However, when the coronavirus pandemic struck in 2020 and most people were confined to their homes, I saw an opportunity for the project to be brought forward – not only to allow it to come to fruition sooner but also to maintain public engagement while IBCC remained closed. It was clear to me that it would also give people something rewarding to occupy themselves during this difficult period. As is invariably the case where IBCC is concerned, the public rose to the challenge admirably and forty volunteers came forward and together spent more than 500 hours recording the epitaphs.

Having already spotted that many of the epitaphs are quotes from poems, hymns and other works of literature, I asked the volunteers to offer some interpretation for as many as they were able, and this has been included in the Losses Database alongside each inscription. This is a vital and unique aspect that sets the database apart from any other site where the epitaphs are recorded, since it offers a much deeper insight into both its meaning and, in many cases, the reasons why it may have been chosen.

As expected, many are not in English and so began the extra task of recruiting volunteer translators for eleven languages, no easy feat when one considers that many were in little-used languages such as Latin. Fortunately, my 'day job' requires frequent contact with my firm's distribution channels throughout the world and my contacts in those organisations provided access to almost all the translations that were necessary.

I also asked the volunteers to highlight the ones they found most moving, and many of the epitaphs featured in this book are the result of that request. That there were so many should come as no surprise; it was the last deed that their families could grant to their beloved son, daughter, husband or wife. Little wonder that a great deal of thought went into them.

What did surprise everyone though is just what variety is to be found amongst them. Some are literary quotes from great works, some quotes from obscure works. Some are school mottos, references to the airman's brothers being lost, or the children they left behind. Some contain cricket references; some even contain gentle humour.

Light features in over 500 Bomber Command epitaphs. A few speak of a light being snuffed out all too soon whereas most speak of light in a positive sense; either God's light continuing to shine upon them or that their memory radiates light upon

those that are left. In all instances, however, the light is portrayed as being constant, everlasting, perpetual.

Garden metaphors, and in particular references to flowers, are frequent too. Some refer to walking in God's garden, others of the flower being plucked too soon, still more of the abiding fragrance long after the flower has been cut.

Similarly, tears are frequently mentioned, sometimes unseen, yet many speak of the tears being wiped away by God. Others demand that no tears be shed, offering up admiration of their honour and bravery by way of alternative.

Understandably, many inscriptions question the meaning of war, whilst others offer hope for the future in a world changed for the better. Perhaps the most poignant ones, however, are the ones penned by the family members who were left behind, or even by the airmen themselves through their last letters.

Without question this has been a deeply insightful and moving odyssey for Steve and myself. There are so many other epitaphs we could have chosen, each equally moving or insightful, often both. We hope it fills you with the same emotions we felt while writing it.

Dave Gilbert, April 2025.

Introduction

By Steve Darlow

'Regret to Inform You'

On 24 June 1944, in Beech Hill, Wigan, a young boy knocked on the door of Kathleen Oliver's house. She answered and he handed her a telegram. It was from the Officer Commanding 622 Squadron. 'Regret to inform you that your husband 1006958 Sergeant Frederick Oliver is missing as result of air operations on the night of 23/24 June 1944'.[1]

Those four words – 'Regret to inform you'. No one ever wanted to read them. During the Second World War the next of kin of tens of thousands Bomber Command service personnel received telegrams that opened with such simple yet heart wrenching phrases. There may have been slight variations. The telegram to Henry Maudslays' mother opened with 'Deeply regret to inform you', Henry having failed to return from the raid on the German dams on 16/17 May 1943.[2] The telegram to the mother of Canadian Jack Fitzgerald opened with 'Regret to advise', Jack having been reported missing from a minelaying sortie on the night of 26/27 August 1944.[3] Whatever words opened the telegram, the impact was the same. In 1947 Kathleen Oliver wrote the poem Telegram Boy, '… please pedal slowly, let them dream two minutes more, for their dreams will die for ever, when you knock upon their door.'

The dreaded 'missing' telegram could only give brief information. The respective casualty may have been killed in an accident, in which case there was no hope, but most of the telegrams were not so final, in stating that the casualty was 'missing' as a result of air operations. Anxious families were desperate for further news, and for many the wait for the next official correspondence was short. A letter from the commanding officer of the respective squadron or station would quickly follow, usually opening with commiserations, then commenting on the good character of the airman and brief details about the operation.

Wing Commander Garner at RAF Kirmington wrote of Jack Fitzgerald, 'Your son was a most proficient Air Gunner … I would like you to know how greatly we all honour the sacrifice he has made so far from his home country in the service of the United Nations. His loss is sadly felt by us all.' Wing Commander Swales DFC DFM, commanding No. 622 Squadron wrote to Fred Oliver's wife, 'He was the Mid Upper Gunner on an aircraft engaged on an important bombing mission over enemy territory, and after take-off nothing further was heard. It is possible that the aircraft was forced down, and if this is the case there is some chance that he may be safe and a

Prisoner of War. In this event it may be two to three months before any certain information is obtained through the International Red Cross.'

These letters rarely, if at all, commented on the specific fate of the casualty. At this stage they simply did not know. News of whether or not the airman was alive or dead could take weeks, months, or even years. Until that confirmation, families clung on to the hope that perhaps their boy, or their husband, may be hiding in occupied territory, or that they had been captured, in which case at least they were alive. History now tells us, however, that the odds were against survival. Four-fifths of those who failed to return from Bomber Command operations were killed.

The scale of Bomber Command losses during the Second World War escalated in line with the expansion of the force, and the number of operational sorties. The principle causes being enemy action (flak, then fighter aircraft) and weather. The official history *The Strategic Air Offensive Against Germany 1939-1945* provides the following in regard aircraft missing on operations.[4]

Year	Total Despatched	Total Missing	Percentage
1939	333	33	9.9%
1940	20809	494	2.4%
1941	30608	914	3.0%
1942	35050	1400	4.0%
1943	64528	2314	3.6%
1944	148448	2573	1.7%
1945	64738	597	0.9%
TOTAL	364514	8325	2.3%

The numbers of men in each of the respective aircraft varied. In the early years it could be three men in a Bristol Blenheim, or four in a Handley Page Hampden. Five in an Armstrong Whitworth Whitley, and five, often six men in the Vickers Wellington. Then through 1942 and into 1943, when the four-engine Short Stirlings, Handley Page Halifaxes, or Avro Lancasters progressively took up the majority of front-line duties they would be manned by seven, sometimes eight airmen. As the war progressed the annual number of individuals lost rose from three-figures to four-figures to five figures, placing great demands on the bureaucracies set up to administer the processing of casualties.

Shortly after the start of the Second World War a dedicated casualty branch was established within the Air Ministry. Named P4(Cas) the branch's personnel set about collating information concerning missing Royal Air Force personnel. For losses over enemy territory information from the International Red Cross would arrive concerning the specific fate of airmen, drawn from enemy sources such as German 'Totenlisten', with details of deaths and places of burial. On 4 August 1944, six weeks after her husband had gone missing, the Air Ministry wrote to Fred Oliver's wife Kathleen, informing her that with deep regret, 'a telegram has been received from the International Red Cross Committee, quoting German information.' It went on to state that five of her husband's crew had been captured and, 'two members, whose identity the German authorities are unable to establish at present, belonging to the crew of this Lancaster aircraft, lost their lives on that date.' The letter continued, 'it would unhappily appear that your husband is one of the two unidentified members referred to as having lost their lives.'

With the escalation of the air war and the corresponding rise in casualty numbers, a 'Missing Research Section' was formed within P4(Cas). Once the Allied armies had established themselves in Western Europe, following the June 1944 Normandy invasion, a team was sent to France that December, and the 'Missing Research and Enquiry Service' (MRES) formed the following year. The task was clear, to research and enquire 'in liberated territories and those occupied by Allied forces, into the circumstances of air crews reported missing of whom no previous trace has been found. The service will also endeavour to obtain additional information to supplement that already received.'[5] The numbers were immense, almost 42,000 RAF personnel reported as missing. Not all those listed, however, had any chance of being found, with thousands lost over the sea, so the expectation required of the MRES was revised to 25,200.[6]

It soon became apparent that an organisational rethink was needed, and the initial eight Missing Research Sections were replaced by four larger Missing Research and Enquiry Units (MREUs) covering Western and Central Europe, with a fifth MREU to cover Southern Europe and the Mediterranean. (Missing research activities were also conducted in the Far East.) The MREUs, in addition to researching the fate of the missing, also set about identifying the graves of airmen who had been buried by enemy forces or the liberating Allied armies, or by local friendly civilians. Such was the case in regard Jack Fitzgerald. In June 1946 the Royal Canadian Air Force were able to share information with Jack's mother. 'A report has been received from the Royal Air Force Missing Research and Enquiry Service on the Continent giving the results of their investigations concerning the fate of your son'. The letter gave details about the final flight, and information concerning the crash from Danish eyewitnesses, and how the entire crew were interred in a communal grave. 'The reverend care of the burial places of all who served in the Forces of the British Empire is the task of the Imperial War Graves Commission. Already eminent architects are at work, planning the construction of beautiful cemeteries and each individual grave will be supported and sustained by the nations of the Empire. I hope that it may be of some consolation to you to know that your gallant son's grave is in sacred care and keeping.'

Established by Royal Charter on 21 May 1917, during the First World War, the Imperial War Graves Commission's commemoration of the war dead only really began after the Armistice. The army, in dealing with an unprecedented number of war dead, had established a non-repatriation rule, and the government decided that those in isolated graves and makeshift burial grounds should be exhumed and concentrated in larger cemeteries.[7] There would also need to be agreement on the design and uniformity of graves. These policies were, at the time, and as the Commission's history states, 'hotly contested'.[8]

In a House of Commons debate of 4 May 1920, Sir James Remnant argued, 'that the relations of the dead should have the right, within properly defined limits, as to size, taste, design, expense, and even of material to be used, to erect what headstones they like as representative of the personality of the individual, and as a personal tribute of affection to their own dead'.[9] Winston Churchill in response,

(Letter sent to the mother of Bomber Command air gunner Aubrey Read.)

Tel.: Bourne End 594.

IMPERIAL WAR GRAVES COMMISSION,
WOOBURN HOUSE, WOOBURN GREEN,
HIGH WYCOMBE, BUCKS.

20 OCT 1950

Dear Sir or Madam,

I venture to ask for your assistance in completing the attached form.

The Imperial War Graves Commission have been entrusted, for this war as for the last, with the duty of permanently commemorating those members of His Majesty's Naval, Military and Air Forces from all parts of the British Empire who die in the service of the Allied cause. The Commission will consequently be responsible for marking and caring for the graves, or, in the case of those who have no known grave, for making provision for other suitable form of commemoration and also for recording all names in permanent Registers. This work will be carried out at the cost of the Commission, whose funds are provided by all the Governments of the Empire.

A headstone of the same simple pattern will, as before, mark each grave; thus every man, rich or poor, General or Private, will be honoured in the same way.

In order to carry out these duties, and to complete the permanent Registers, the Commission desire certain additional information which they hope you will be so good as to supply on the attached form, which should then be returned to the Commission.

You will notice that a space has been left on the form for a personal inscription to be selected by the relatives, if they so desire, for engraving on the headstone. Where, owing to the course of military operations, it has so far been impossible to find or identify a grave, no personal inscription should be inserted on the form. Should the grave eventually be discovered, I shall, of course, write to you again, and you will then have a further opportunity to choose an inscription.

Some relatives have expressed the wish to pay for this personal inscription, and an opportunity will be given to them later on of meeting the cost. Should they not wish to do so, the cost will be borne by the Commission.

Owing to increase in the cost of engraving Personal Inscriptions since the attached form was printed, the amount which may be paid by relatives has been raised from 7s. 6d. to £1.

Yours faithfully,
F. HIGGINSON,
Secretary.

(5141/3188) Wt. P.0082/3575 30m. 4/49 T. & B. Gp. 468

commenting on the scale and practicalities of the Commission's task remarked that this would result in extra complexity and 'you would not get these graveyards finished within the lifetime of the present generation.' The design would remain uniform, albeit with relatives having a say on the personal inscriptions. One other government policy would also remain contentious, particularly in respect of those lost in the Second World War, the repatriation of bodies buried in Germany, the land of the enemy.

With the breakout of hostilities in 1939 the Commission prepared, again, for a considerable number of war dead to commemorate. In the United Kingdom either existing IWGC plots were extended or the military authorities and civilian authorities agreed on new locations. Brookwood Military Cemetery, which came into being in 1917, was extended during the Second

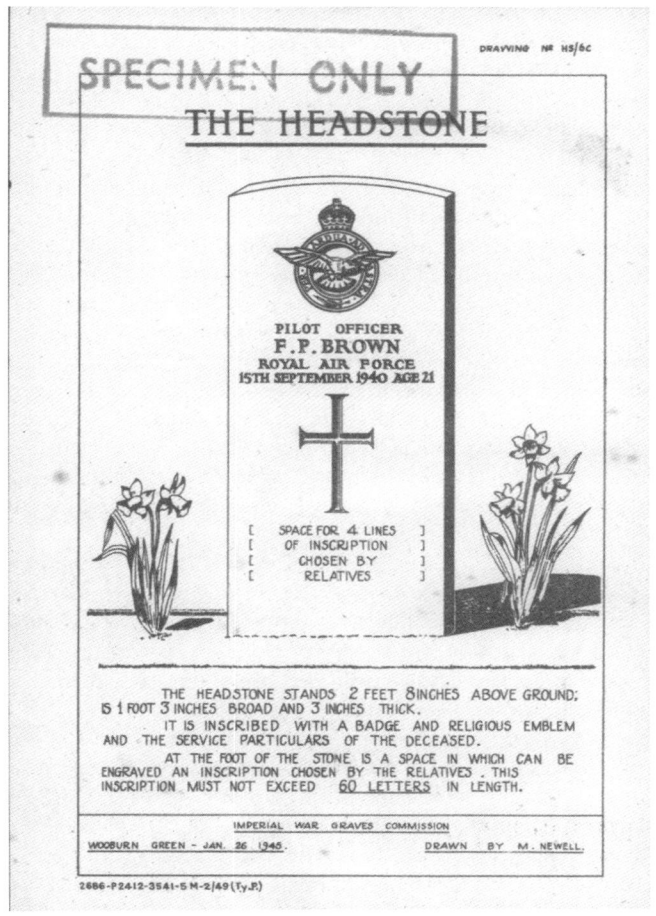

World war, and is now the largest Commonwealth war cemetery in the UK, with a considerable number of air force graves. Of the 988 Second World War burials at Harrogate (Stonefall) Cemetery, virtually all are of men who served in nearby bomber stations, two-thirds being Canadians. Early in the war a part of the cemetery was allotted, and in July 1943 the Air Forces Section opened.[10] A considerable number of British nationals, however, would be returned to local parish cemeteries. Cambridge City Cemetery already held war dead from the First World War when a further plot was added in 1940, along with the Air Force plot in 1942. Many of the graves at Cambridge hold men lost on the night of 16/17 December 1943, when, on return from a raid on Berlin, numerous aircraft crashed trying to find their base in thick fog. Piloting a No. 405 Squadron Lancaster was Canadian Burns

McLennan, who now rests in the cemetery, with his fellow Canadian crewmates (Epitaph: I HAVE FOUGHT A GOOD FIGHT, I HAVE FINISHED MY COURSE, I HAVE KEPT THE FAITH). The body of McLennan's British flight engineer, Herbert Cornwell was taken back to his home village, and he rests in Bottisham cemetery (Epitaph: AT THE GOING DOWN OF THE SUN AND IN THE MORNING WE WILL REMEMBER HIM).

When it came to airmen buried overseas, there were two main approaches. In the countries liberated by the Allies the graves of airmen carefully tended by sympathetic locals were left undisturbed, with the commission's employees and contractors caring for the graves after the war. Jack Fitzgerald still rests with his crew in Gammell Rye Churchyard, Denmark, and Frederick Oliver is buried in Socx Churchyard, France. In hostile countries, such as Germany itself, such care and attention may have been unlikely, although this was not always the case, as is detailed in regard some of the war dead featuring in this book. Nevertheless, bodies were exhumed from their initial burial locations and reinterred in large cemeteries, for more efficient and effective commemoration, and to be maintained 'in perpetuity' by the IWGC. The body of Henry Maudslay, having initially been buried in the Nord Friedhof, Düsseldorf, was reburied, amongst almost four thousand of his Bomber Command colleagues, gathered from all over western Germany, in the Reichswald Forest War Cemetery.

Whether the airmen had been buried in hostile or friendly countries, the graves were usually marked with a simple cross, using various types of materials, sometimes pieces of the aircraft. The cross marking the grave of Jack Fitzgerald's crew was forged by the locals from a piece of the spar recovered from his crashed Lancaster.

In the spirit of equality, these would need to be replaced, in line with one of the key policies adopted but the IWGC, the uniformity of the headstone. These should be a consistent size and shape, and each headstone would then display details respective to the casualty. In regard Bomber Command, at the top the respective air force crest, then their military details including rank, name, and date of death. Finally, at the base, a personal inscription submitted by the family, the epitaph, taken from a 'Final Verification Form' that had been returned to the IWGC by the next-of-kin. (The government of New Zealand, in the aftermath of the First World War, fearing a perception of inequality, decided against allowing personal inscriptions. A policy maintained after the Second World War, ensuring no discrimination between the treatment of their dead.) The form stated that the families were allowed a maximum of sixty letters[11], although, as apparent in the following pages, many epitaphs exceeded the sixty-letter limit, the IWGC adopting the approach that they would, if possible, accommodate such requests to avoid further upset.

And so it was that Kathleen Oliver had sixty characters to express the sense of grief and loss felt by her and the family. Kathleen decided upon A TOKEN OF LOVE AND REMEMBRANCE. HIS MEMORY HELD EVER DEAR. Henry Maudslay's mother submitted HE DIED GLORIOUSLY IN THE BREACHING OF THE EDER DAM. For Jack Fitzgerald, his family chose LOVE AND REMEMBRANCE LAST FOREVER.

Steve Darlow, April 2025

Cambridge City Cemetery

IT'S NOT THE WORDS, THEY ARE SO FEW, BUT THE MEMORIES WE KEEP OF YOU

AIRCRAFTMAN 1ST CLASS ERNEST WILLIAM LYON
WIRELESS OPERATOR/AIR GUNNER (RAF), NO. 107 SQUADRON
DIED 4TH SEPTEMBER 1939, AGED 19
BURIED SAGE WAR CEMETERY, GERMANY

The No. 107 Squadron Operations Record Book entry for 3 September 1939 reads, 'After a state of tension lasting several days, War was declared on Germany. The Squadron was ordered to mobilise and change to its War establishment.' The following day's entry would open with, 'Five aircraft left to attack a German warship at Wilhelmshaven Harbour.'[12] That day RAF Bomber Command suffered its first casualties of the conflict, with seven aircraft lost, including almost all the No. 107 Squadron Blenheims – only a solitary aircraft returning safely. Of the four that had taken off from RAF Wattisham and failed to return, two men were captured, and ten men lost their lives, including Ernest Lyon. Although flying on a No. 107 Squadron Blenheim that day, Ernest was on loan from No. 110 Squadron, which is the squadron number shown on the Commonwealth War Graves Commission site.

Ernest was originally buried in Wilhelmshaven cemetery, next to observer Owen Howells and near pilot Herbert Lightoller. In July 1947 No. 74 Graves Concentration Unit exhumed Ernest's body, which was wrapped in a parachute, from the grave marked with a cross showing 'Engl. Flieger William Lyon'. The exhumation report noted an other ranks service dress, a wireless operator flash, leather flying boots and other ranks issue socks, all of which was consistent with it being Ernest's body. A positive identification had been made and arrangements were set in place to remove and rebury Ernest, along with the bodies of his pilot and observer. In May 1949 Ernest's father received a letter from the Air Ministry Casualty Branch.[13]

> Dear Mr Lyon,
> I am writing to let you know that a report has been received from the Royal Air Force Missing Research and Enquiry Service, stating that the grave of your son … has been removed to the British Military Cemetery at Oldenburg (Sage), where he now rests … The reburial is in accordance with the policy agreed by His Majesty's and the Commonwealth Governments, that our fallen should be transferred to specially selected military cemeteries where the graves will be maintained, for all time, by the Imperial War Graves Commission.

WHEN DUTY WHISPERS LOW, THOU MUST, THE YOUTH REPLIES, I CAN

SERGEANT CHARLES GEORGE WILLIAMS
AIR GUNNER (RAF), NO. 144 SQUADRON
DIED 29TH SEPTEMBER 1939, AGED 19
BURIED SAGE WAR CEMETERY, GERMANY

This inscription is taken from the third stanza of a lengthy 1863 poem entitled *Voluntaries* by American essayist, poet and philosopher Ralph Waldo Emerson. Written to bolster dwindling enlistment as the American Civil War dragged on, it is surprisingly only quoted in three Bomber Command epitaphs.[14] The full stanza reads as follows:

> In an age of fops and toys,
> Wanting wisdom, void of right,
> Who shall nerve heroic boys
> To hazard all in Freedom's fight,—
> Break sharply off their jolly games,
> Forsake their comrades gay,
> And quit proud homes and youthful dames,
> For famine, toil, and fray?
> Yet on the nimble air benign
> Speed nimbler messages,
> That waft the breath of grace divine
> To hearts in sloth and ease.
> So nigh is grandeur to our dust,
> So near is God to man,
> When duty whispers low, Thou must,
> The youth replies, I can.

Charles Williams was a pre-war regular and was raised in the Bristol suburb of Westbury-on-Trym. On 29 September his aircraft, together with four others, took off from RAF Hemswell, Lincolnshire to reconnoitre and bomb in broad daylight shipping in Heligoland Bight. Disastrously, not a single one returned, each having been shot down by fighters. Of the twenty airmen who took part, sixteen perished and four would be incarcerated for the full duration of the war. No. 144 Squadron's motto 'Who shall stop us?' must have seemed rather ironic.

Still predisposed to former British Prime Minister Stanley Baldwin's doctrine that 'the bomber will always get through', Bomber Command flew operations by day, but the Battle of Heligoland Bight some three months later would change all of that. On 18 December, twenty-four aircraft took off to attack capital ships anchored off Wilhelmshaven. The bomber force was met with an overwhelming response of forty-four German fighters, many with recent combat experience obtained during the Spanish Civil War. Of the twenty-two bombers that reached the target, twelve were shot down with the loss of fifty-seven airmen for only two fighter losses.

FREEDOM IS THE SURE POSSESSION OF THOSE ALONE WITH COURAGE TO DEFEND IT

PILOT OFFICER HORACE MIERS MACGREGOR
PILOT (RAF), NO. 7 SQUADRON
DIED 1ST JANUARY 1940, AGED 19
BURIED HARROW (PINNER) CEMETERY, UNITED KINGDOM

The epitaph is a quote from *Pericles Funeral Oration*, taken from historian Thucydides's *History of the Peloponnesian War*. Remembering and honouring the war dead, the famed and eminent Athenian statesman Pericles chose to recognise heroic sacrifice. Freedom was not something that could be taken for granted. Once attained it belonged to those who had the physical and mental courage to protect it from threat. The war dead in 'choosing to die resisting, rather than to live submitting', and 'having judged that to be happy means to be free, and to be free means to be brave', did not shy away from the risks of war. The Pericles quote was also chosen to feature on the rear of the plinth carrying the aircrew statues at the Bomber Command Memorial in The Green Park, London. Although there is a slight difference with John Branton's epitaph in that 'with' has replaced 'who have the'. Perhaps to ensure that the epitaph fell within the sixty letter war graves commission limit.

On the morning of New Years Day 1940, whilst carrying out a navigational exercise, Horace, in trying to lift his Handley Page Hampden above cloud, crashed into Snaefell, Isle of Man. Horace and two of his crew were killed.[15] Corporal Ted Brightmore, the only survivor, would later recall, 'I remember a terrific thump and tearing sound, being drenched in petrol, a big explosion, rolling into some snow which must have put out my personal fire and saved my life.'[16] Seriously burnt and struggling through the snow, Ted eventually reached a farmhouse.

When news reached RAF Jurby at 2pm, 300 airmen along with several civilians were organised into a search party, and two hours later the aircraft was found, wrecked and completely burnt out.[17]

For Ted Brightmore a long period in hospital followed, including burns treatment by Dr Archibald McIndoe. Fifty-five years after the fateful day Ted met with a member of the rescue party, who had contracted pneumonia during the search, and a Mrs Cottier, who lived at the farmhouse, and together they laid a wreath at the crash site.[18]

HE WAS THE FIRST OF THREE TO FALL

SERGEANT JOHN ROYAL BRANTON
OBSERVER (RAF), NO. 226 SQUADRON
DIED 7TH APRIL 1940, AGED 27
BURIED TERLINCTHUN BRITISH CEMETERY, WIMILLE, FRANCE

No. 226 Squadron, operating Fairey Battle light bombers, had been deployed to France early in the war, as part of the Advanced Air Striking Force. On 8 April 1940, Sergeant W.A. Dunn reported.[19]

> On the night of the 7/4/40 I was detailed to carry out a night X-country flight in Battle P 2265. The Observer was Sgt. Branton and the Wireless Operator was Lac. Davies. At approximately 21.55 hours when flying on an even keel, the aircraft suddenly went into a steep climb. On pushing the control column forward the engine cut out and the machine went out of control. I gave the order for the crew to jump (3 times) at about 3.000 feet. I remained in the machine trying to correct it, but the engine would not pick up. At 900 feet I jumped by parachute.

John Branton and Percy Davies lost their lives and rest side by side in Terlinchthun British Cemetery.

Many of the epitaphs on the graves of Bomber Command airmen reference other family members lost in the conflict. The 'Three' mentioned in the epitaph above include John's brothers Jacob and Leonard. The 1921 census shows that John Royal Branton (age 7), and Leonard (age 5) and Jacob (age 1) were living with their parents William and Lydia, and seven other siblings in the parish of Eston, Middlesbrough. Lydia, whose maiden name was Royal, would pass away three years later and William would remarry, Elizabeth Barnes, in 1931. (On the Commonwealth War Graves Commission site John and Leonard are showing as the sons of William and Lydia, and Jacob as the son of William and Elisabeth.)

Ordinary Seaman Jacob Branton lost his life serving with the escort carrier *HMS Begum* on 6 July 1944 and is buried in Trincomalee War Cemetery, Sri Lanka. His grave bears the inscription 'FOR HOME AND COUNTRY'. Sergeant Leonard Branton lost his life on 27 April 1942 and is buried in Basingstoke (Worting Road) Cemetery. The husband of Ida Branton there is no epitaph displayed on his grave. Leonard was killed in a Spitfire accident flying with No. 1 Photographic Reconnaissance Unit.

TO HIS GLORIOUS MEMORY. AT REST WITH HIS THREE BROTHERS. "THY WILL BE DONE"

FLYING OFFICER DONALD EDWARD GARLAND VC
PILOT (RAF), NO. 12 SQUADRON
DIED 12TH MAY 1940, AGED 21
BURIED HEVERLEE WAR CEMETERY, BELGIUM

As one of only twenty-six Victoria Cross winners in the RAF, much has been written about Donald Garland. Born in County Wicklow, Ireland on 28 June 1918, his family later moved to East Finchley, where he and his brothers were educated at the well-regarded Cardinal Vaughan Memorial School.[20] On leaving, Donald worked in an insurance office before enlisting with a short-term commission. After training he was posted to No. 12 Squadron, at that time part of the Advanced Air Striking Force, based at Amifontaine, France.

Until his fateful sortie, he had been tasked with a few 'Nickel' raids – propaganda leaflet drops – but nothing directly in the face of the enemy. That changed on 12 May 1940 when the squadron was required to attack two newly established enemy positions on bridges over the Albert Kanaal in Belgium. The attack needed to be in daylight for maximum precision, and the Germans had by then had enough time to set up flak batteries and establish fighter circuits. It was considered so dangerous that the commanding officer asked for volunteers. Every crew put themselves forward. They were equipped with Fairey Battle aircraft, a hopelessly obsolete marque even at the beginning of the war, which had won the unenviable epithet 'flying coffin' due to its slow speed and limited range.

Garland led the attack comprising six aircraft – three to attack each bridge. As expected, they experienced a hail of anti-aircraft fire. Fighter escort was provided, although so overwhelming was the number of enemy fighters that they were of little benefit. Garland and his wing-men approached at low level, putting themselves in easy range of enemy machine guns. Despite the ferocity of the oncoming fire, they succeeded in dropping their bombs at one end of the bridge seconds before plunging into the ground. The bridge partly collapsed, preventing enemy vehicles from crossing, for a while at least.

Garland and his crew were secretly buried by local people, the site later being disclosed to the Allies, who re-interred them at Lanaken, then Heverlee War Cemetery. Whilst Garland and his observer Thomas Gray each received the VC, the gunner LAC Reynolds received no recognition, something that continues to be perceived as an injustice.

Tragically, all three of Donald's brothers were lost in the service of the RAF, hence the wording of his epitaph. It is difficult to comprehend the sense of loss that their parents Patrick and Winifred must have felt.

WAVING GOODBYE TO ME SMILING COURAGEOUSLY
YOUR LIFE YOU GAVE SO YOUNG AND FREE

AIRCRAFTMAN 1ST CLASS SYDNEY MARTIN
WIRELESS OPERATOR/AIR GUNNER (RAF), NO. 150 SQUADRON
DIED 14TH MAY 1940
BURIED DOUZY COMMUNAL CEMETERY, FRANCE

The epitaph chosen by Sydney's wife Jean certainly evokes a picture. A young man about to leave for war, smiling at this wife, perhaps wanting to allay any fears she undoubtedly had. Fears that were realised, as it proved a final goodbye, with Jean choosing to remember her husband as someone who had given his life.

In May 1940 Sydney was with No. 150 Squadron, in France, operating as part of the Advanced Air Striking Force. On the tenth of the month Germany launched its offensive in the West, crossing into Belgium and Holland, advancing rapidly over the coming days. Attempting to arrest the developing Blitzkrieg, the RAF called on their Fairey Battle crews to attack enemy ground forces. It was a day of great courage. It was a day of terrible loss with thirty-one Battles shot down including that of Sydney, with no survivors from the crew of three.

When Flight Lieutenant Aptroot of No. 2 Section, No. 1 Missing Research and Enquiry Unit visited Douzy Communal Cemetery in November 1946 he was told by the cemetery keeper that although shown as a communal grave all three members of the crew, Sydney, pilot John Boon, and observer Thomas Fortune were in separate coffins.[21] Sydney, Thomas, and John were originally buried close to where their bodies were discovered, and by plotting the places where the crew were found, Aptroot discovered the remains of the Fairey Battle. With the original location of the bodies in a straight line from the crash site, Aptroot surmised each of the three airmen must have tried to leave the aircraft at the final moment, with John Boon the last to exit. An exhumation was ordered with the intention of discovering the identity of the bodies in each of the coffins.

At the end of January 1947, the grave was opened, and although there were indeed three coffins, the central coffin was found to contain the remains of more than one airman. As such Sydney's, John's, and Thomas' final resting place remains recorded as a communal grave.

ALL YOU HAD HOPED FOR, ALL YOU HAD, YOU GAVE.
LOVINGLY AND PROUDLY REMEMBERED

SERGEANT CECIL ERNEST COLBOURN
OBSERVER (RAF), NO. 15 (B) SQUADRON
DIED 18TH MAY 1940, AGED 26
BURIED LANDRECIES COMMUNAL CEMETERY, FRANCE

Sergeant Colbourn was killed in the desperate days shortly before the fall of France, during which the German advance was so rapid that the British needed to quickly retreat to successive airfields before eventually evacuating to England, often just moments before the German Panzers reached them.

By this point XV (B) Squadron was no longer part of the Advanced Air Striking Force, having returned to RAF Wyton in early 1940 to re-equip with Bristol Blenheim aircraft and to engage in attacks on roads and bridges in an effort to halt the Panzers' advance. Flown mainly during daylight hours, their task was perilous, and the losses sustained were dreadful. On this occasion they were due to rendezvous with fighter escorts, which failed to appear.

Unsurprisingly given the circumstances, the records kept by the squadron were brief. Cecil is listed just twice in the squadron records – once for an attack on bridges at Maastricht on 12 May (see also Flying Officer Donald Garland VC) and again three days later on his fateful operation.[22]

Six Blenheims were tasked with attacking enemy transport approaching Le Cateau and destroying the bridge they were heading toward. Anti-aircraft fire was heavy and enemy fighter activity intense. Of the six aircraft that set out, three failed to return and another was written off due to damage sustained during the attack. Eight of the eighteen airmen were killed and one became a prisoner of war. Clearly, a loss rate of 50% per attack was unsustainable, even for a short period of time.

It is not clear whether Sergeant Colbourn's aircraft, captained by Flight Lieutenant Paul Chapman, was brought down by flak or by a fighter. It crashed near Landrecies, killing all three airmen. They were laid to rest in the local cemetery.[23]

Cecil was twenty-six-years-old and left grieving parents Charles and Gertrude and wife Jean of Winchmore Hill, Middlesex. His epitaph is an excerpt from the poem and hymn *O Valiant Hearts*, written by Sir John Stanhope Arkwright and set to music by Charles Harris. It features on some thirty-eight Bomber Command epitaphs and other excerpts of the same hymn are quoted on more than a hundred others (see also the Tod brothers).

OF WITHAM, ESSEX "GARDE TA FOY"

FLYING OFFICER HENRY GEORGE EVITT
PILOT (RAF), NO. 88 (HONG KONG) SQUADRON
DIED 29TH MAY 1940, AGED 26
BURIED CHOLOY WAR CEMETERY, FRANCE

Henry, or George as he was known to many, was born on 5 May 1914 at Witham, Essex to Henry and Susannah, the youngest of four siblings. His father was a farmer and a stocks and shares dealer.[24]

No. 88 Squadron was, at the time of his death, part of the Advanced Air Striking Force of the British Expeditionary Force and had already fallen back to safer airfields as the Germans advanced. On the day of this, his fateful sortie, they were stationed at Les Grandes Chappelles and were tasked with night-time bombing of a fuel storage depot in the Givet region. The Squadron ORB, characteristically brief for the period and circumstances in which it was written, merely states that all three of the crew were killed when 'one bomb onboard the aircraft exploded'.[25] In fact, the bomb exploded shortly after take-off, although it is unclear whether this was the cause or result of the crash.

They were laid to rest in Troyes Cemetery, although in 1950 they were moved (or 'concentrated' in Imperial War Graves Commission parlance) to Choloy, where they rest in consecutive graves. Grave concentration was routine, the purpose being to ensure that their graves could be maintained in perpetuity.

A matter of days after the crash, No. 88 Squadron would evacuate back to England.

Henry's epitaph, which might at first sight appear to be in Latin, is in fact Old French and translates as 'Keep Your Faith'. It is famously the motto of Magdalene College, Cambridge and since Henry was old enough to have graduated, enquiries were made of Magdalene's alumni officer to no avail, although it is also the motto of several schools, one of which is Felsted Independent School in Essex. It is clear from his epitaph that Witham was his hometown, a matter of only five miles from Felsted, and further enquiries confirmed that it was indeed his alma mater, between 1924 and 1931.

His entry in the school obituary reads 'George will be remembered by his contemporaries as a rather diminutive person, who made up for his lack of stature by his cheerfulness and large heartedness. On leaving school he studied chemistry and later managed a fruit farm. He received a short service commission in the RAF in 1938 and was killed in action in June [sic] 1940.'[26]

TREAD GENTLY O'ER THIS AIRMAN'S GRAVE.
A MOTHER'S LOVE LIES HERE. HIS WIDOWED MOTHER

SERGEANT JAMES PATTERSON
WIRELESS OPERATOR/AIR GUNNER (RAF), NO. 102 (CEYLON) SQUADRON
DIED 17TH AUGUST 1940, AGED 20
BURIED KLAGENFURT WAR CEMETERY, AUSTRIA

On 7 August 1946 Frau Mariaberta Ploner wrote to the Air Ministry, and a translation of the letter is in the respective casualty file.[27] Mariaberter and her husband Rupert were the caretakers of the Göppingerhütte, in the Alps, near Lech, Arlberg, Austria.

> In reply to your letter dated 11th July, I will give you the following details regarding the tragic end of the Wellington bomber crew.
>
> I was able to find out that Friedrichshafen was attacked and owing to very heavy Flak fire the formation was broken up and the bomber driven off to the Great Walsertal; the weather on that day was very bad and a snow storm raged in the Alps. The aircraft probably completely lost its bearings, and drifted through clouds in the snowstorm, looking for a possibility to land, since, below the scene of crash there, actually was a large green plain where the aircraft could have made a perfect landing; instead, the poor things had the misfortune to graze the Schuchenwand a spur of the Hochlichtspitze, breaking off one wing, and crashed from a height of 60-80 metres over a precipice. The crew and the bomber were found after 8 days by tourists, who reported the crash to the authorities without telling us a word about it. Had we known my husband could have recovered some personal effects of the airmen, which he could have now sent to their families.
>
> We are terribly sorry not to have seen the aircraft crash, as we could have gone to their aid immediately, but the aircraft crashed at 0200 hours at night, during a snowstorm, which drowned any other sounds. You can rest assured that we would have helped gladly.
>
> After 8 days, 12 Rural Policemen, 1 Captain and 2 Sentries arrived, the next day 10-12 Riflemen from Sonthofen, Bavaria, came to recover the dead, further a Commission of Engineers and a Demolition Detachment from Berlin.
>
> I personally asked the captain, a Tyrolese, to take the dead to our hut, which he did, and they were buried one minute's walk from the hut.
>
> My husband arranged the grave well and every year when spring was on its way, I decorated the grave with flowers. We were very fond of our dead comrades, but now they were taken from us and transported to Klagenfurt (apparently there is a large British cemetery there). We shall put up a memorial to the dead and always keep them in memory.

SO DID HE JOIN THE CHOIR INVISIBLE
WHOSE MUSIC IS THE GLADNESS OF THE WORLD

SERGEANT FREDERICK WALTER NOAKES
AIR GUNNER (RAFVR), NO. 38 SQUADRON
DIED 11TH SEPTEMBER 1940, AGED 23
BURIED OOSTENDE NEW COMMUNAL CEMETERY, BELGIUM

On 8 September 1940 orders came through at No. 38 Squadron, 'from HQ No. 3 Group that we were standing by Alert No.1; the invasion is imminent, all on leave recalled.'[28] With intelligence reports of a build-up of German shipping in Channel coastal ports, notably invasion barges, and backed up by photographic reconnaissance, Bomber Command was called upon to intervene. On the morning of 11 September, No. 38 Squadron initially detailed eleven aircraft to attack German targets but late in the day the objective for five of the squadron's Wellingtons, including that of Fred Noakes and his pilot F/O Allen, was changed to Ostend. The squadron diary would later record that 'F/O Allen, it is regretted, and his crew have not returned, it is possible they may have forced landed in Belgium territory.'

In June, 1942, Frederick's father received a letter from the Air Ministry informing him that, 'as a result of enquiries made through the International Red Cross Committee, Geneva, which states that the aircraft in which your son, Sergeant Frederick Walter Noakes, 902559, lost his life, was shot down … and that the six members of the crew were buried in the military section of the municipal cemetery, Ostend. The report states that only three of the crew were able to be identified, and unfortunately your son was not one of these.'[29]

In January 1946 a search officer from No. 2 Missing Research and Enquiry Unit visited Ostend New Cemetery and noted that wireless operator/air gunner James Johnstone, and pilots Richard Allen, Charles Dufton were buried in ground 9B Row 3, graves 31,34, and 35 respectively. The three unknowns were buried in ground 9b, row 3 grave 32 and 33 and row 4, grave 1. An exhumation, carried out in November, revealed it was impossible to identify the unknowns, and that as one of these graves was in a separate row to the others, row 4, grave 1, a decision was made to exchange these remains with that of James Johnstone, so the unknowns could have a collective grave.

Frederick Noakes is now recorded as resting in collective grave 31-33, with wireless operator/air gunner Charles Matthews and observer Eric James.

OUR BELOVED DENNIS. HE BELIEVED IN ENGLAND AND DIED TO KEEP HER FREE. MOTHER

SERGEANT CHARLES DENNIS GAVIN
OBSERVER (RAF), NO. 105 SQUADRON
DIED 15TH NOVEMBER 1940, AGED 23
BURIED BRUSSELS TOWN CEMETERY, BELGIUM

On the evening of 14 November 1940 No. 105 Squadron despatched seven Blenheims to attack Luftwaffe airfields. Intelligence was warning of a major raid on a UK target, and later that night over 500 German bombers would cause widespread death and destruction in the city of Coventry. At 1910 hours the Blenheim flown by Dennis Murray, with Charles Gavin as Observer, and Thomas Robson as the wireless operator/air gunner took off from RAF Swanton Morley, although icing prevented them attacking their allotted airfield and they attacked Boulogne instead.

The next day, No. 2 Group instructed No. 105 Squadron to prepare for a maximum effort in the Antwerp – Brussels Le Culot – St. Trond area, maintaining attacks on enemy aerodromes, 'with a view to hampering operations and preventing aircraft from leaving the ground'.[30] As it was, of the nine Blenheims crews that were briefed only four took off, owing to deteriorating weather. One of these was Charles Gavin's, acting in direct defence of his home country. Taking off at 1925 hours the crew failed to return. Those that did make it back to Swanton Morley reported, 'seeing tracer bullets from an aircraft making a very low attack in the vicinity of Dieghem. This aircraft was engaged by the ground defences and was seen to crash in flames. It was later reported by the German High Command that Pilot Officer Murray, and his crew, Sergeant Gavin and Sergeant Robson had been killed in action.'

Initially buried in three graves, only that of Thomas Robson bore a cross with his name. The other two graves were marked 'unknown' although bearing the same date as that of Robson's marker. Despite an exhumation it was not possible to definitively distinguish between the remains of Charles and Dennis Murray and their final resting place was marked as a joint grave, albeit with a misspelling of Charles' surname as 'Garvin' which would be rectified on the Imperial War Graves Commission headstone.[31]

In the epitaph Charles Dennis Gavin is referred to as Dennis, no doubt owing to his father being called Charles. The epitaph, however, appears to have been submitted just by Dennis' mother Anne, referencing her son's patriotism, with his country, at that time of his death, under direct attack.

DEARLY LOVED HUSBAND OF ALICE ELLIS
REUNITED 29TH MAY 1995

SERGEANT HYLTON DANIEL ELLIS
OBSERVER (RAF), NO. 115 SQUADRON
DIED 9TH DECEMBER 1940, AGED 26
BURIED NORTH GOSFORTH JOINT BURIAL GROUND, UNITED KINGDOM

By December 1940, although the threat of an enemy invasion had diminished considerably, Bomber Command was still tasked with deterring any further German intentions, targeting channel ports and airfields. On 8 December 1940 nine crews of No. 115 Squadron were detailed to attack Bordeaux and Lorient, including that of Hylton Ellis. Having taken off at 1715 hours from RAF Marham the Wellington crashed into high ground at Cefn-y-strad, near Tredegar, Gwent, in the early hours of 9 December.[32] There is now a cairn and cross with an inscribed metal plaque at the crash site.

On 21 April 1941 Hylton's wife Alice wrote to the Air Ministry, asking if a gravestone could be erected to mark his grave.[33]

> I have information from a friend of mine whose husband was killed on active service in the RFC in the last war that the Air Ministry (or its equivalent then) very kindly erected a gravestone for her. Does this apply now, because if so I should very much like it that way, showing that he belonged to the RAF – he was so proud of that fact.

The Director or Personal Services replied, 'the Imperial War Graves Commission is empowered to maintain war graves in this country. Their intention is, at the cessation of hostilities, to erect memorials similar to those placed on the graves of the men who died in the last war. In the meantime the graves will be marked with a white wooden cross.' Alice responded.

> After fully considering the proposal of the Air Ministry to erect a white wooden cross now, and after the war a memorial, I feel I would like a proper memorial erected now. I fully realise that it would not be possible for the Air Ministry to undertake this work now. But, I'm quite willing to see about the erection of a memorial myself and wondered if the Air Ministry would be willing to help defray the cost … May I request an early answer as I'd like to hasten the erection of the memorial for the anniversary of my husband's death.

On 9 October, Alice received a letter stating that, 'with regret there are no air force funds from which grants can be made towards the erection of private memorials.'

(Alice would subsequently marry Hylton's brother William. In September 1945 William, a pilot, arrived at No. 33 Squadron based at Sylt, the squadron diary reporting 'Sgt Ellis, carrying out his first trip with the squadron collided on one of the air to ground firing targets … crashing on to the beach and disintegrating into the sea.' William rests in Kiel War Cemetery.[34])

BELOVED SON OF J.&A. COATES, ROSSENDALE, LANCS., ENGLAND
"HIJ STIERF OPDAT GIJ VRIJ ZOUDT ZIJN"

SERGEANT JACK COATES
WIRELESS OPERATOR/AIR GUNNER (RAF), NO. 114 (HONG KONG) SQUADRON
DIED 31ST DECEMBER 1940, AGED 19
BURIED BERGEN-OP-ZOOM WAR CEMETERY, NETHERLANDS

Translation from Dutch
HE DIED THAT YOU MIGHT BE FREE

This epitaph is an unusual mix of English and Dutch and has clearly been created by Jack's loved ones with the intention of directly addressing local people in the Dutch cemetery in which Jack is buried. Its meaning will not have been lost on those local people; Dutch remembrance is as impressive as it is widespread, often involving placing candles on each grave on Christmas Eve. In 2024, the Lichtjes op Oorlogsgraven (Lights on War Graves) project, as it is called, took place across 482 locations in Belgium and the Netherlands, during which some 25,740 war graves were lit up.[35]

Jack Coates arrived at No. 114 Squadron, RAF Oulton, from No. 42 Operational Training Unit on 29 December 1940. He must scarcely have had time to unpack his kit bag before his first operation just two days later on New Year's Eve. Five crews were stood by for a battle order to attack enemy aerodromes and industrial targets, provided there was good cloud cover. One of the Mk. IV Bristol Blenheim aircraft was detailed for a weather recce in the morning and after reporting favourable conditions back to base, went on to bomb oil storage tanks at Vlaardigen.[36]

Having established that the weather conditions were indeed favourable, two of the remaining aircraft set off just before noon for an attack on the Gilze-Rijen and Berck-sur-Mer aerodromes in southern Holland and France respectively. Jack's aircraft was detailed for Gilze-Rijen close to the Belgian border, which had been used by the Luftwaffe since the Germans advanced through the Low Countries in May.

At 1420 hours, the aircraft was bombarded by the flak guns at Gilze as it approached the target and it crashed at De Moer, exploding as it hit the ground and killing all three on board. Jack was just nineteen years of age and John and Annie, his parents, must have been devastated by their loss, which was most likely conveyed to them by telegram on New Year's Day 1941.

"IF YE BREAK FAITH WITH US WHO DIE WE SHALL NOT SLEEP, THOUGH POPPIES GROW"

SERGEANT HAROLD GORDON
OBSERVER (RAFVR), NO. 58 SQUADRON
DIED 3RD MARCH 1941, AGED 23
BURIED HARDENHUISH (ST. NICHOLAS) CHURCHYARD, UNITED KINGDOM

Harold's family have drawn upon the poem *In Flanders Fields* written by Canadian John McCrae in May 1915 whilst serving as a physician and soldier during the First World War. McCrae presided over the burial of a close friend and having seen how poppies grew around the graves of dead soldiers, articulated his feelings in a poem which to this day features prominently in Remembrance services and commemorations. Writing from the viewpoint of those who had fallen – 'We are the Dead' – McCrae's words implore the reader to honour their sacrifice and continue the fight. The last stanza reads

> Take up our quarrel with the foe:
> To you from failing hands we throw
> The torch; be yours to hold it high.
> If ye break faith with us who die
> We shall not sleep, though poppies grow
> In Flanders fields.

Harold's Whitley was one of eight aircraft sent by No. 58 Squadron to take part in an attack on enemy warships at Brest on the night of 2/3 March 1941. Having taken off from RAF Linton-on-Ouse just after 6pm, the crew signalled, ten minutes before midnight, that the operation had been abandoned. Indeed, one other 58 Squadron crew would later report, 'owing to 10/10 cloud unable to locate the primary or any other target. Bombs jettisoned in sea', and another crew 'unable to locate primary target' brought their bombs back to Linton.

A few minutes before 2am Harold's Whitley crashed near Ternhill, Shropshire with a total loss of life. Harold was taken to his parent's hometown of Chippenham and buried on 10 March in Hardenhuish (St Nicholas) Churchyard. Similarly, the rest of his crew were buried in cemeteries local to their parent's homes.

GOD GAVE US MEMORY SO THAT WE MIGHT HAVE ROSES IN DECEMBER

SERGEANT CECIL NORMAN WELLER
OBSERVER (RAFVR), NO. 20 OPERATIONAL TRAINING UNIT
DIED 15TH MAY 1941, AGED 20
BURIED LOSSIEMOUTH BURIAL GROUND, UNITED KINGDOM

In *Courage - The Rectorial Address Delivered at St. Andrews University May 3, 1922* the Scottish playwright and novelist James M. Barrie opens with,

> You have had many rectors here in St. Andrews who will continue in bloom long after the lowly ones such as I am are dead and rotten and forgotten. They are the roses in December; you remember someone said that God gave us memory so that we might have roses in December.[37]

James Barrie's fame was already well established, having written *Peter Pan, or The Boy Who Wouldn't Grow Up*. (Bringing to mind the line from poem *For the Fallen* by Laurence Binyon, 'They shall grow not old'.) Barrie's use of the 'Roses in December' metaphor suggests even the darkest of times can be illuminated by God's gift of memory. And what greater darkness can there be than the passing of a child. Cecil was the son of Joseph and Alice Weller and let us hope their 'roses' did bring some solace.

Cecil was part of a crew of six that took off from RAF Lossiemouth on 15 May. The flying accident report concluded that the primary cause of the Anson crashing, which came down 3 miles east of Banff, was that it had stalled at a low height, with a secondary cause being the prevalent snow storm.[38]

There was a total loss of life on the Anson. Cecil was laid to rest in Lossiemouth Burial Ground, alongside fellow observer, Canadian Joseph Brissenden (EVER REMEMBERED, EVER LOVED). Observer Bertram Headland was buried in Tottenham Cemetery (no epitaph), wireless operator/air gunner Edward Hughes was buried in Stoke-on-Trent (Hanley) Cemetery (GREATER LOVE HATH NO MAN THAN THIS, THAT A MAN LAY DOWN HIS LIFE FOR HIS FRIENDS). Wireless operator/air gunner Harold King rests in Brighouse Cemetery (HE GAVE HIS LIFE THAT WE MIGHT LIVE "LET PERPETUAL LIGHT SHINE UPON HIM" R.I.P.) and pilot Howard Thomas lies in Penarth Cemetery (IN LOVING REMEMBRANCE).

"DON'T WORRY: I AM ALRIGHT"

SERGEANT FRANK WOOD
PILOT (RAFVR), NO. 18 (BURMA) SQUADRON
DIED 25TH MAY 1941, AGED 19
BURIED LEMVIG CEMETERY, DENMARK

Brief yet poignant, this epitaph is another most likely penned by the airman himself as part of a last letter to loved ones.

Although Coastal Command were mainly responsible for mine-laying and maritime patrol duties, it was not uncommon for Bomber Command to be similarly tasked, particularly in the early years of the war.

Frank hailed from Ford, near Aylesbury in Buckinghamshire. Since his arrival at No. 18 (Burma) Squadron, RAF Oulton, he had flown nothing but maritime reconnaissance and shipping attack sorties. This was his tenth 'op.', in which he and his crew were tasked with a daylight patrol of 'Beat 10' along with five other aircraft.

During the patrol they, along with two other Blenheim aircraft from the same unit, attacked a 1500-ton cargo vessel flying the Nazi flag. All three aircraft approached the target but one of them had a bomb hang-up so failed to press home his attack.

The other two, including Sergeant Wood, succeeded in bombing the target but came under light anti-aircraft fire and his aircraft was seen to be hit in the starboard engine, which caught fire. The aircraft crashed in flames a few metres out to sea on the west coast of Denmark, near Vrist.[39] The wireless operator/air gunner, Sergeant Cyril Norman Harris, survived with minor injuries and was picked up by a Danish fishing boat, becoming a prisoner of war.[40]

Frank and his observer, Sergeant Ernest George Baker were laid to rest in consecutive graves at Lemvig Cemetery. Ernest's gravestone inscription simply reads HAPPY MEMORIES.

IN PROUD & CONSTANT MEMORY OF A GALLANT ENGLISHMAN WHO GAVE HIS LIFE TO SAVE HIS CREW

WING COMMANDER ROY GEORGE CLARINGBOULD ARNOLD
PILOT (RAF), NO. 9 (IX) SQUADRON
DIED 9TH JUNE 1941, AGED 30
BURIED BLANKENBERGE TOWN CEMETERY, BELGIUM

It is often said that air gunners occupied the most vulnerable positions in a bomber and there is no doubt that their lot was a cold and lonely one. The rear gunner was particularly exposed, as enemy night fighters usually approached from the rear; however, statistically speaking, theirs was not the deadliest of trades.

Rather, the pilot was the most likely to be killed for the simple reason that, as captain of their aircraft, they would remain at the controls for as long as possible to ensure the rest of the crew could make good their escape. By the time their own opportunity came, the aircraft was often too low for their parachute to be effective, or the aircraft was already starting to disintegrate.

There are countless examples of crews surviving because of the actions of their captains and perhaps that's why crews held their skipper in such high regard. Quite simply, they knew he would be prepared to pay the ultimate price to save them.

Roy was a pre-war regular with the RAF, having enlisted in 1931, and had risen to be commanding officer of No. 9 Squadron at RAF Honington. He had been brought up in the *Kent Hotel*, a popular spot for holidaymakers on the sea front at Margate.

He would occasionally fly with scratch crews, often made up of 'spare bods' – airmen who had no regular crew for a variety of reasons, such as having flown insufficient ops to be screened, when their crewmates had. This was one such occasion when, on 9 June 1941, he led the squadron on a daylight operation: a low-level armed reconnaissance along the French and Belgian coast.[41] They were attacked by three Me109s and set on fire. Recognising that the situation was hopeless he ordered his crew to abandon while he remained at the controls. The Wellington bomber crashed near Zeebrugge, killing Roy.[42]

His crew included two senior officers in the squadron, navigation leader Flying Officer Dominic Bruce and gunnery leader Flying Officer Tom Bax. Bruce, already holder of an Air Force Medal, became known for his numerous escape attempts which resulted in him eventually being sent to Colditz.[43] After the war he was one of the few airmen to receive a Military Cross.[44] Roy is also remembered on the Margate War Memorial. His old home is still there, now renamed *The Flamingo*.

HE SERVED ONLY SIX WEEKS BUT HE GAVE ALL.
SOME DAY WE'LL UNDERSTAND

AIRCRAFTMAN 2ND CLASS ERNEST ALFRED FIDELL
(RAFVR), NO. 7 SQUADRON
DIED 23RD JULY 1941, AGED 20
BURIED ARNOLD CEMETERY, UNITED KINGDOM

At the time of his passing Ernest Fidell was serving at RAF Oakington, the home of Bomber Command's No. 7 Squadron. The Operations Record Book for 23 July notes, 'A few small bombs 8 were dropped in the early hours of the morning near the Squadron offices. One other rank of the Ground Defence was killed and slight damage done to Stirling T. N6032 by bomb splinters.'[45] That 'other rank' was Ernest.

Ernest's parents James and Edith came from West Bridgford, Nottingham and their son's body was taken to Arnold Cemetery, a few miles north-east of Nottingham, for burial.

At the time of submitting the epitaph to the Imperial War Graves Commission, it appears that James and Edith wanted to specifically express a hope that eventually the reason for the loss of their boy would become clear.

"I AM A JEW"

SERGEANT ISRAEL JACOBOVITCH (ALIAS: SERGEANT HAROLD JACKSON)
WIRELESS OPERATOR/AIR GUNNER (RAFVR), NO. 50 SQUADRON
DIED 12TH JULY 1941, AGED 25
BURIED VEENDAM GENERAL CEMETERY, NETHERLANDS

The simplest of inscriptions, yet one of the most powerful, encapsulating in just four short words the entirety of his motivation to fight. Because the permanent headstones were placed some while after the end of the conflict, the full horrors of the holocaust would by then have been laid bare and, in choosing this epitaph, it is clear his parents wished to make a bold statement.

The son of a tailor from the predominantly Jewish neighbourhood of West Hampstead, London, Israel Jacobovitch clearly understood the risks if he were to be captured by the Germans and so served under the alias Harold Jackson, although his father had listed him in the 1939 census by that name, so it was more than simply a nom de guerre. So complete was his alias that his true identity was not discovered until after the end of the Second World War.

Israel was born in London on 29 May 1915 to Isaac and Miriam (née Bernstein). He had two older siblings, Anne and Jack. Isaac had been working as the manager of a radio shop whereas Jack was the manager of a china shop.[46]

He arrived at RAF Lindholme from No. 14 OTU on 3 July 1941. Just ten days later he would be dead, having flown three operations: Mönchengladbach, Köln and Bremen.[47] Their aircraft, a Mk. I Handley Page Hampden, was shot down on the outward leg by a Messerschmitt Bf 110 night fighter flown by Oberleutnant Helmut Lent from unit 4./NJG 1, based at Leeuwarden.[48] The crew of four all perished when it crashed just before 1pm at Veensloot, east of Groningen. The captain, Pilot Officer Edward Vivian, hailed from Johannesburg and the wireless operator, Flight Sergeant Jack Guest, had received the honour of the British Empire Medal in 1938 when he returned to his crashed and burning aircraft to save two of his fellow crew.[49, 50]

'TIS NOT THE DUTY OF THE DAY THE RACE YOU HAVE TO RUN BUT THE THING YOU NEEDN'T DO EARNS THE GREAT "WELL DONE"

SERGEANT JAMES TINKER
WIRELESS OPERATOR/AIR GUNNER (RAFVR), NO. 17 OTU
DIED 12TH JULY 1941, AGED 21
BURIED RAMSEY CEMETERY, CAMBRIDGESHIRE, UNITED KINGDOM.

Another inscription which is unique amongst Bomber Command epitaphs and, while appearing to be a quote from a famous literary work, there is no evidence of that. There's little doubt that it is a reference to the fact that he, like all RAF aircrew, was a volunteer.

Jim was born in the industrial Don Valley area of Sheffield on 5 February 1920, one of four children, and had been employed as a clerk at a firm of accountants.[51]

On Saturday 12 July 1941, he and two other airmen took off from RAF Wyton en-route to nearby RAF Upwood in a Mk. IV Bristol Blenheim to practice landings with wireless assistance. The pilot, Sergeant Ronald Smith, lost control and failed to recover from a spin before crashing at Old Halves, near Chatteris, Cambridgeshire with the loss of all aboard.

In his last letter home to his sister Betty, sent the day before he was killed, he told her that he had just finished his air gunnery course and was due to move on to an operational training unit any day. He signed off with 'Your loving brother – Jim. P.S. don't write here again, I shall probably have left'.[52] How poignant that must have seemed in hindsight.

A memorial to this and six other aircraft that crashed in the Chatteris area may be found adjacent to the town's war memorial.[53]

INTO THE MOSAIC OF VICTORY
WAS PLACED THIS PRECIOUS PIECE

SERGEANT GEORGE HAINES
WIRELESS OPERATOR/AIR GUNNER (RAFVR), NO. 51 SQUADRON
DIED 7TH AUGUST 1941, AGED 25
BURIED EINDHOVEN (WOENSEL) GENERAL CEMETERY, NETHERLANDS

There are many subtle variations on this popular epitaph, which appears on sixty-six Bomber Command headstones. Some state 'he placed his precious piece', whereas others emphasise the sacrifice made by the airman's family by using 'we place this precious piece'.[54] Either way, this epitaph speaks of the collective sacrifice of all those lost during the conflict, each being an individual yet inseparable part of the mosaic.

The exact origin of this fitting inscription is unknown, although it doesn't appear to be associated with First World War epitaphs.

George was born in Stapleford, Nottinghamshire on 23 December 1915 to James and Mary Haines and had been employed as a progress clerk before enlisting. He flew his first operation at No. 51 Squadron on 5 May 1941 against Mannheim. By 6 August he had taken part in fourteen attacks, mostly on well defended German cities. He had flown with a variety of skippers, including Wing Commander Burnett, the squadron commanding officer, who went on to hold a number of very senior post-war roles including Vice Chief of the Air Staff.

On 6/7 August, the target for the night was Frankfurt, an eight-hour round trip for the crew of five in their Armstrong Whitworth Whitley medium bomber. Fifty-three aircraft had been detailed for this target, of which four failed to return, including George's.[55,56] It was attacked by Hauptmann Werner Streib at 0215 hours, sending the stricken bomber down at Heeze, south-east of Eindhoven.[57] All the crew initially survived but George was badly wounded and died some hours later in a German hospital.

Streib was already an experienced ace with eighteen victories to his name and by the end of the war had some sixty-eight credits, including an extremely rare 'ace-in-a-day' when he shot down five heavy bombers on 12 June 1943 as they attacked Düsseldorf.[58]

NON NOBIS SOLUM SED TOTI MUNDO NATI

SERGEANT HENRY BRUCE STIRLING JOHNSTON
OBSERVER (RAFVR), NO. 9 (IX) SQUADRON
DIED 20TH AUGUST 1941, AGED 21
BURIED TONDER CEMETERY, DENMARK

Translation from Latin
NOT FOR OURSELVES BUT FOR THE WHOLE WORLD BORN

An adaptation of a quotation from Cicero's *De Officiis*, this expression was adopted by many schools as their motto, perhaps most famously by Liverpool Institute after it was used as the title and lyric of a 1990s oratorio written by Sir Paul McCartney about the school that he and George Harrison attended.[59]

Bruce Johnston, however, attended Wellingborough School in Northamptonshire, which uses *Salus in Arduis* (Latin: Fulfilment through Challenge) as its motto[60], so it was likely chosen by his parents Robert and Kathleen for entirely different reasons.

When Bruce, who was known by his middle name, left Wellingborough School in 1935, aged 15, he joined the National Provincial Bank (now part of Natwest plc) as a probationer at the Weymouth branch. He was promoted to clerk in April 1939 but a little over a year later, after volunteering for the RAFVR, he was called up for service.[61]

On 19 August 1941 Bruce and his crew were detailed for an attack on railway targets in the German port city of Kiel. Hit by flak at 0035 hours, they crashed just off the Danish coast with the loss of all six crew members. (The Commonwealth War Graves Commission website shows a date of death of 19 August. However, the aircraft crashed after midnight, so we have used the date of 20 August above.) Bruce and the crew were buried in consecutive graves in Tonder Cemetery with full military honours, including a Wehrmacht band, although strangely not until almost two months later, on 23 October.[62]

Tragically, Bruce's parents had already lost an elder son just five weeks earlier. Pilot Officer Robert Alan Johnston of No. 611 Squadron was killed when his Spitfire was believed shot down in the St. Omer area of France during a 'Circus Operation' (light and medium bombers escorted by fighters). Alan, as he was known, was laid to rest in Pihen-lès-Guînes Communal Cemetery and his headstone bears the same inscription as Bruce's.

Their names may also be found on a memorial in the Church of St. Peters, Portesham, Dorset and on a memorial erected by their aunt in Putney Vale Cemetery.

YOUR HAPPY SMILE IS WITH US ALWAYS.
GOOD NIGHT, CHAS., TILL A BRIGHTER DAWN

SERGEANT CHARLES ALFRED TRACEY
PILOT (RAFVR), NO. 18 (BURMA) SQUADRON
DIED 16TH SEPTEMBER 1941, AGED 24
BURIED TEXEL (DEN BURG) CEMETERY, NETHERLANDS

On 19 September 1941 Wing Commander D.C. Smythe, commanding No. 18 Squadron, wrote to Charles' father.[63]

> I deeply regret to inform you that your son was reported missing from operations on the afternoon of the 16 September.
>
> Yous son was leading a formation which was searching for reporting vessels in the North Sea, and he had completed his beat and was on his way home flying at very low altitude in order to escape detection by any enemy warning system. The Air Gunner of the other aircraft which was with him suddenly noticed your son's aircraft hit the sea. The aircraft rose again and the Gunner thought that your son had got his aircraft under control, but it lost height again and was seen to go into the sea. The other aircraft immediately turned and circled over the spot where your son's aircraft went in, but they could see no wreckage or any sign of any survivors … search aircraft were sent out immediately, but although they searched the area they were unable to find any survivors and I am afraid that I think it is highly unlikely that any members of the crew can have survived.
>
> Your son had been with the squadron for some time now, and had completed a number of very successful operational missions. He had shown outstanding promise, and I had every intention of recommending him for a commission in the hope of one day having him as one of my Flight Commanders.

Subsequently a Dutch Red Cross report stated that Charles' body washed ashore at Texel on 1 November and he was buried in the municipal cemetery at Den Burg.

The English Hymnal published in 1906 is a hymn book devised by Anglican priest Percy Dearmer and composer Ralph Vaughan Williams. Included is the hymn with the following opening stanza

> A brighter dawn is breaking,
> And earth with praise is waking;
> For thou, O King most highest,
> The power of death defiest;

Charles Tracey's family may also have drawn on one of the translations of the Bible's Proverbs 4:18, for example, 'But the path of the righteous is like the light of dawn, which shines brighter and brighter until full day.'

TO LIVE IN THE HEARTS OF THOSE WE LOVE IS NOT TO DIE

PILOT OFFICER JAMES CLARENCE HOWELL
PILOT (RAFVR), NO. 58 SQUADRON
DIED 19TH SEPTEMBER 1941, AGED 30
BURIED BERLIN 1939-1945 WAR CEMETERY, GERMANY

James' epitaph is taken from the poem *Hallowed Ground* by the Scottish writer, and author of patriotic war poems, Thomas Campbell (1777–1844). The epitaph is presumably chosen by James' wife Kathleen, expressing the sentiment that her husband remains part of her, and therefore lives on. The second stanza of the poem reads.

> That's hallowed ground where, mourned and missed,
> The lips repose our love has kissed;
> But where's their memory's mansion? Is 't
> Yon churchyard's bowers?
> No! in ourselves their souls exist,
> A part of ours.

And the third stanza, from which the epitaph is taken, reads.

> But strew his ashes to the wind
> Whose sword or voice has served mankind,
> And is he dead, whose glorious mind
> Lifts thine on high?
> To live in hearts we leave behind
> Is not to die.

No. 58 Squadron sent five of their Whitleys to raid Stettin on the night of 19/20 September 1941, a round trip of almost ten hours. Three crews reported attacking their primary target and a fourth claimed to have bombed Parow aerodrome. The squadron diary recorded for James Howell's Whitley that, 'No word received from this aircraft since leaving base. Three aircraft report having seen supposed aircraft coming down in flames Rostock area between 0230 and 0250 hours. Aircraft presumed missing with crew.' James' Whitley had indeed crashed, near Warnemünde.[64] Three of the crew were found on the airfield and two, including James, fell into the sea. James' body was the last to be recovered, on 31 October and four days later he was buried with military honours, next to his crewmates in the new cemetery in Rostock. A wreath with the inscription 'Die Deutsche Luftwaffe' was laid on his grave. After the war it took some time for the Russians to grant permission to a MREU team to visit the cemetery and in April 1947 James and his four colleagues were exhumed, easily identified, and taken to what was then called Heerstrasse British War Cemetery (now Berlin 1939-1945 War Cemetery), where he now rests side by side with his colleagues.

In the casualty file for this crew there is a letter, dated 27 July 1947, from the mother of air gunner Thomas Wood, in which she says she was 'very glad to know he is now resting in British soil.' Thomas' epitaph reads PEACE, PERFECT PEACE, WITH LOVED ONES FAR AWAY?

Berlin 1939 - 1945 War Cemetery

Of the 3,595 Commonwealth burials approximately eighty per cent are airmen.

ONE CROWDED HOUR OF GLORIOUS LIFE
IS WORTH AN AGE WITHOUT A NAME R.I.P.

SERGEANT BERNARD KENNETH GEORGE WILLMER
WIRELESS OPERATOR/AIR GUNNER (RAFVR), NO. 104 SQUADRON
DIED 27TH SEPTEMBER 1941, AGED 20
BURIED EXETER HIGHER CEMETERY, UNITED KINGDOM

Although sometimes attributed to Sir Walter Scott, this epitaph is in fact an excerpt from the oft-quoted poem *The Call* by Major Thomas Osbert Mordaunt (1730–1809). Mordaunt was from a long line of high-ranking soldiers, some of whom also entered politics. Scott had in fact merely quoted one stanza in his novel *Old Mortality*.

The full poem runs to fourteen stanzas but the stanza in question reads as follows:

> Sound, sound the clarion, fill the fife!
> Throughout the sensual world proclaim,
> One crowded hour of glorious life
> Is worth an age without a name.

Bernard Willmer had arrived at No. 104 Squadron at RAF Driffield in the East Riding of Yorkshire on 6 September 1941. On 27 September, a crew made up mostly of freshers, but with a more experienced pilot and wireless operator, were sent to RAF Exeter to collect a repaired aircraft which had been damaged by flak during an attack on Brest harbour at the beginning of July.[65] The starboard engine had failed as a result of the flak damage, necessitating an early landing, most likely because the pilot found himself unable to maintain sufficient altitude to be confident of making it back to Driffield.

Prior to making the trip back to base, the crew took the Wellington up for an air test. It is not certain exactly what happened during the test but the aircraft crashed two miles north-east of the airfield with the loss of all on board. Some of the airmen were returned to their families for burial and the rest, including Bernard and the Canadian captain, Pilot Officer John Robertson, were buried locally. Robertson's inscription reads TOO DEARLY LOVED TO BE FORGOTTEN.

Four of the crew, including Bernard, went to their graves without flying a single operation.

YOU CANNOT PASS BEYOND OUR BOUNDLESS LOVE

PILOT OFFICER EDGAR GORDON SMITH
PILOT (RAFVR), NO. 77 SQUADRON
DIED 30TH SEPTEMBER 1941, AGED 20
BURIED KIEL WAR CEMETERY, GERMANY

Edgar's family have chosen a quote from the poem *Christ's All!* by John Oxenham, the Manchester born poet writing under a pseudonym, his real name being William Arthur Dunkerley. Oxenham's optimistic and hopeful poems struck a chord with the population during the First World War. In writing about 'our boys who have gone to the front' he wishes to portray them as not being like Christ, but being Christ, 'For they have gone, most of them, from a simple, high sense of duty, and in many cases under direst feeling of personal repulsion against the whole ghastly business. They have sacrificed everything, knowing full well that many of them will never return to us.'[66] Lines in the poem express the value of this sacrifice, including, 'Ye are all christs in this your self-surrender', and 'This mighty work to which your souls are set.' The final stanza of the poem reads

> O Lads! Dear Lads! Our Christs of God's anointing!
> Press on in hope! Your faith and courage prove!
> Pass-by these High Ways of the Lord's appointing!
> You cannot pass beyond our boundless love.

Accompanying Edgar Smith on his Whitley for the long flight to Stettin on the night of 29/30 September 1941 were two fellow British nationals Alan Pedley and Ronald Dunkley, and Canadians John Hiltz and Harold McColm. The casualty file for the crew[67] provides an eye witness report stating Edgar's Whitley 'was shot down by flak batteries at approximately 0200 hours … The aircraft was burning in mid-air and eventually crashed in the district known at Flem-Moor. Immediately in reaching the ground a large explosion followed … All of the crew were killed.' In July 1948 Edgar's father received a letter from the Air Ministry.

I am very sorry to renew your grief in the loss of your son, Pilot Officer E.G. Smith, but I am sure you will wish to know that the Royal Air Force Missing Research and Enquiry Service operating in Germany have reported that his remains have been removed from the Kiel Garrison Cemetery and reverently re-interred, together with three of his crew companions, in a comrades' group of graves number 2 to 5 in Row J, Plot III of the British Military Cemetery at Kiel. Sergeant McColn [sic], the only member of the crew whom it was possible individually to identify, prior to reburial, rests in a grave nearby.

PAULATIM ERGO CERTE
"SUNSET AND EVENING STAR AND ONE CLEAR CALL FOR ME"

SERGEANT JOSEPH ERNEST MEDHURST
OBSERVER (RAFVR), NO. 57 SQUADRON
DIED 11TH OCTOBER 1941, AGED 19
BURIED RHEINBERG WAR CEMETERY, GERMANY

Translation from Latin
SLOWLY THEREFORE SURELY

This inscription is an unusual combination of Latin and English. The Latin element is the motto of the highly regarded Latymer School in Hammersmith, London, which Joseph attended between 1933 and 1938. Latymer lost an astounding twenty-six of their alumni to Bomber Command during the Second World War, which they have proudly compiled into a book entitled *The Fallen Latymerians of The Second World War*, along with losses sustained in other services. The publication says of Joseph: '…though a high-spirited and cheerful boy [he] was nicknamed rather inaptly 'The Mouse'. He left school without matriculating, but won the junior half mile in 1937. 'The Mouse' enjoyed every minute of his short but happy life, and his Latymer days, he said, were the happiest of all.'

The English element of the inscription is an excerpt from *Crossing the Bar* by Alfred, Lord Tennyson, which was later set to music as a hymn. The full poem reads as follows:

Sunset and evening star,
And one clear call for me!
And may there be no moaning of the bar,
When I put out to sea,

But such a tide as moving seems asleep,
Too full for sound and foam,
When that which drew from out the boundless deep
Turns again home.

Twilight and evening bell,
And after that the dark!
And may there be no sadness of farewell,
When I embark;

For tho' from out our bourne of Time and Place
The flood may bear me far,
I hope to see my Pilot face to face
When I have cross'd the bar.

The penultimate line can easily be interpreted as a juxtaposition of the pilot of an aircraft with God as the ultimate pilot and, unsurprisingly perhaps, it is separately used in thirteen Bomber Command epitaphs.[68]

HERE WE HAVE LIFE
THROUGH YOUR MOST VALIANT DEATH

SERGEANT DONALD AUSTIN WATSON
PILOT (RAFVR), NO. 57 SQUADRON
DIED 11TH DECEMBER 1941, AGED 25
BURIED FELTWELL (ST. NICHOLAS) CHURCHYARD, UNITED KINGDOM

On 11 December 1941 Donald Watson's crew was one of five at No. 57 Squadron detailed to carry out a raid on Le Havre. Two of the returning crews reported that they were 'unable to locate target'. Donald's Wellington, with a crew of six, had taken off in the late afternoon carrying a bombload of three SBC's (small bomb container) and fourteen 250 pounders. The 'Report of Flying Accident or Landing Not Attributable to Enemy Action' recorded that at 2058 hours Donald's Wellington was heard over East Wretham and a request was made to land. 'No reply was given and at 2100 hours it crashed two miles from East Wretham. All the crew were killed and the aircraft completely destroyed.' It appears that Donald's crew were similarly 'unable to locate target' as all the bombs were found in the wreckage. 'The weather at the time was good. Sufficient petrol was carried for a further two and a half flying hours.'[69] Donald's body was later identified by his position in the aircraft and identity discs, and he was buried in Feltwell on 16 December.

Also buried in Feltwell is pilot Philip Gurd (A HANDSOME AND BRAVE, SPIRITED YOUNG CHAP WHO DIED FOR HIS COUNTRY) and wireless operator/air gunner John McKenzie (HE DIED FOR FREEDOM AND THE RIGHT). Observer Edwin Carter is buried in Chislehurst Cemetery (O FOR THE TOUCH OF A VANISHED HAND AND THE SOUND OF A VOICE THAT IS STILL). Wireless operator/air gunner Stanley Jackson is buried in Dukinfield Cemetery and air gunner Ranulph Mainwaring is buried in Brenchley (All Saints) Churchyard.

Donald's parents, George and Marguerite, were from Jersey, and perhaps the 'here we have life' in the epitaph is a reference to the fact that the Channel Islands were under German occupation for almost five years, coming to an end owing to the sacrifice made by their son. Or perhaps it asks the reader of the epitaph, on Donald's headstone in the United Kingdom, to be thankful that Donald and his colleagues ensured the mainland was never invaded.

"BUT THE APPLE PETALS, WHEN THEY FELL, WERE WHITE"

PILOT OFFICER ANTHONY DAVID SCOTT-MARTIN
PILOT (RAFVR), NO. 77 SQUADRON
DIED 27TH DECEMBER 1941, AGED 20
BURIED RHEINBERG WAR CEMETERY, GERMANY

Although this inscription, which speaks so eloquently of the purity of those who fell prematurely, sounds as though it may have come from a great literary work, there is no evidence to support that presumption. Despite being similar in nature to several works by the American poet Robert Frost (particularly *Putting in the Seed*), none contains this line. Rather, it appears it may have been written by Anthony's parents, perhaps inspired by Frost's works.

Anthony came from the Surrey town of Hurley and was the twenty-year-old son of Paul and Edith Scott-Martin. He had arrived at No. 77 Squadron, which at the time was flying ageing Whitleys, in June 1941. In the six months that followed he had racked up some twenty-seven operations and so was close to achieving a full tour of thirty ops before being screened. Had he achieved it, he would most likely have become a pilot instructor at a training unit.

On 27 December the squadron was tasked with bombing Düsseldorf. Little did they know how disastrous the attack would turn out to be for No. 77 in particular. Twelve aircraft were detailed, although two did not take off for various technical reasons. Of the ten that did, three failed to return with the others all landing away from home base.[70] In all, Bomber Command sent 132 aircraft, yet achieved only superficial damage to the city.[71]

There was at least some consolation for No. 77 when they later learned from the International Red Cross that five of the fifteen airmen lost that night had become prisoners of war. Sadly, none of them were aboard Anthony's aircraft.

Whilst Anthony's epitaph may possibly have been inspired by Robert Frost, it in turn inspired one of the authors of this very book to pen a poem which was included in one of three new Rolls of Honour in Lincoln Cathedral. The original books, presented to the Cathedral in the 1950s, formed the starting point for the IBCC Losses Database and it was quickly discovered that they contained many errors. Dave recreated the books in 2019 and included the following verse in the Training Units book:

> Seldom did the sweet fragrance endure
> so long after the storm had
> dispersed the blossom.

TO YOU WHO ARE LEFT BEHIND IS A TASK . . .
CREATE A NEW ORDER SO ALL MAY LIVE IN PEACE

FLIGHT SERGEANT REGINALD FRANCIS ROBB
PILOT (RCAF), NO. 158 SQUADRON
DIED 26TH FEBRUARY 1942, AGED 25
BURIED BARMBY-ON-THE-MOOR (ST. CATHERINE) CHURCHYARD,
UNITED KINGDOM

Reginald Robb was born 11 June 1916 in Dunnville, Ontario, the son of Walter and Elizabeth. Walter was a county court judge in the Dufferin area, northwest of Toronto. After leaving school, Reg worked as a truck driver for the Orangeville Bottling Works while studying at the University of Toronto, where he gained an Honours degree before becoming a wage clerk at the Bata Shoe Company.[72]

Enlisting on 20 September 1940 he listed golf, tennis, hockey and swimming amongst his pastimes in his attestation papers, which describe him as 'a splendid type for commissioned rank'.

On 26 February 1942, he and his crew were tasked with an operational flight to bomb Kiel. They took off from RAF Pocklington, which they were using temporarily while construction work was being carried out at their home base, RAF Driffield. One of the engines of their twin-engine Wellington caught fire immediately after they became airborne, as a result of which they failed to gain height.[73] Realising they needed to lose weight to stand a chance of going around to make a forced-landing, they jettisoned their load but were caught in the blast of their own bombs, causing Reg to lose control. The aircraft crashed close to the village of Yapham with the loss of all on board. One of the bombs failed to detonate and lay undiscovered until the 1970s when it was found and made safe.[74]

It is not known whether this epitaph was written by Reg himself. A clue may lie in the fact that while at university he majored in English, French, Economics and Psychology. It is clear from his letters home that he was an eloquent writer of prose, an example of which may be found memorialised as a metal plaque in Alexandra Park, Orangeville:

Dear Mom & Dad,
It is the knowledge that there are people at home who are depending on you that drives one not only to do his best, but just a little bit more, and it is this spirit that is going to bring a triumphant conclusion to this struggle in which we are presently engaged. For if we fail then all is lost, not only for ourselves, but for the vast civilized world made up of good people like yourselves. The sacrifice might be great, but it is dwarfed by the magnificent end to which we are pointing.

Your loving son,
Reg.

B'E TAGHADH DO CHUAIRT MAR DH'EUG THU

FLYING OFFICER WESTON JAMES ROBERTSON
WIRELESS OPERATOR/AIR GUNNER (RAFVR), NO. 226 SQUADRON
DIED 26TH MARCH 1942, AGED 33
BURIED MARISSEL FRENCH NATIONAL CEMETERY, BEAUVAIS, FRANCE

Translation from Gaelic[75]
YOU LIVED AS YOU DIED

This is quite a difficult translation as literally it could be 'Your choice of path/journey was as you died'. But the suggestion is that in a more idiomatic sense the epitaph expresses he was someone who lived his life fully, freely, and confidently. He lived as he died, making bold choices and doing what he loved.

On 8 March 1942 twelve Bostons were sent to make a low-level attack on the Ford lorry factory at Poissy, near Paris. The raid was to be led by Wing Commander Vernon Butler DFC, with Flying Officer Basil Sayers and Weston making up the crew of three. An account of what happened on the raid features in author Martin W. Bowman's book *The Reich Intruders: RAF Light Bomber Raids in World War II*[76] Pilot Officer Peter Saunders, flying in another Boston, recalls that the target had been 'decidedly pranged', but then seeing Vernon Butler struggling to close their bomb doors. (In W.R. Chorley's *Royal Air Force Bomber Command Losses* the author notes that the Boston had been damaged by flak and then crippled in the blast from its own bombs.) Peter Saunders looked on, '... could it be the Wingco was hurt? He was still flying skilfully, holding the course, still terrifyingly low. A stretch of thickly wooded ground loomed ahead of us. We swept up and over it. The Wingco's props seemed to trail on the branches below.'

> Without warning it came. His port wing cleaved into a trunk. His aircraft lurched violently ... The Boston tottered, slipped heavily sideways and crashed into the trees. Still on its side, it went hurtling on. Trunks splintered and broke in its path. There was a blinding flash of white-blue flame and then the horror of the scene was cloaked in fierce red fire ... Chappie from his gunner's turret was the only one who could see. He said nothing. Neither could we. We sped homewards.

Vernon Butler and Basil Sayers were killed in the crash. Weston survived but was seriously injured. Taken to the German Air Force local hospital Beauvais, Weston finally succumbed to a streptococcus infection on 26 March. In October 1942 a Letter from the Head of the Wehrmacht Casualties and Prisoners of War Information Bureau in Berlin notified The Prisoners of War Information Bureau in London that Westons' funeral, 'took place during the afternoon of 28th March 1942 with military honours at the French military cemetery Beauvais – Marissel, rue d'Amiens. After the German military chaplain had said a few words the Commandant of a Fliegerhorst laid two wreaths tied with ribbon on the grave and two salvoes were fired.'[77]

SO IMPATIENT, FULL OF ACTION,
FULL OF MANLY PRIDE AND FRIENDSHIP

SERGEANT ERIC DIXON
PILOT (RAFVR), NO. 214 (FEDERATED MALAY STATES) SQUADRON
DIED 2ND APRIL 1942, AGED 20
BURIED RHEINBERG WAR CEMETERY, GERMANY

There can be no mistaking an epitaph written by a mother in her time of grief, and this surely must be one. It can only be hoped that Evelyn Dixon, Eric's mother, and her grieving husband Daniel took some comfort in writing it.

Eric had arrived at RAF Stradishall just before Christmas, 1941. He first flew an operation on 17 December, as second pilot against Le Havre; a largely pointless attack due to 10/10ths cloud cover. Bombing strategic targets in occupied countries relied upon clear conditions since civilian casualties were to be avoided at all costs and crews were almost always ordered to bomb only if they had clear sight of the target, in this case the docks. On this occasion, most crews either jettisoned their bombs in the English Channel or brought them back.[78]

Seventeen ops later, the 1 April 1942 low-level attack on Hanau railway infrastructure was disastrous for No. 214 Squadron. Of the fourteen aircraft detailed, half failed to return. Forty-one airmen killed and one prisoner of war for little strategic or tactical gain. The other squadrons similarly tasked did not fare much better; the total losses for the night amounting to thirty-four per cent.[79]

This had been an experimental attack that Bomber Command would not repeat for reasons that are all too apparent. Arthur 'Bomber' Harris had not long assumed command and changes were going to be made, and made quickly. Only two months later he would initiate the audacious Thousand Bomber Raids (Operation Millennium) against key German cities, the first to use the principle of a bomber stream, which was designed to overwhelm German defensive tactics.

HOME, SULPHUR SPRINGS TEXAS, U.S.A.
UNKNOWN BY HIS COUNTRY, YET WHO GAVE MORE?

PILOT OFFICER WILLIAM STONE TYLER
AIR GUNNER (RCAF), NO. 405 (VANCOUVER) SQUADRON
DIED 15TH APRIL 1942, AGED 21
BURIED RHEINBERG WAR CEMETER, GERMANY

William Tyler's attestation papers make clear his interest in aviation listing against special qualifications and hobbies useful to the RCAF, 'Navigation, cross country flying, drawing, meteorology, aircraft, theory of flight, engines, parachutes, history of aviation, enthusiast radio.'[80] An American citizen from Texas, William's papers, signed at the end of September 1940, showed that prior to the war he had spent time at a Military Academy, with just over forty-five hours flying solo and twenty-nine dual to his name. His interview report noted that he was a 'very good American boy. Should be excellent pilot material', with a further report stating, 'plenty of dash and determination.' Alas, William did not impress the chief flying instructor at No. 7 Elementary Flying Training School, remarking that he 'disregards flying order, had previous flying, difficulty in breaking old habits – too careless to be allowed to continue flying at present.' William's future with the RCAF, unsurprisingly, took a new direction and in April 1941 he was awarded the air gunners badge, serving operationally with No. 35 Squadron then No. 405 Squadron.

On 14 April 1942 No. 405 Squadron detailed six Wellington crews for a raid to Dortmund, and the following day the squadron diary recorded that 'This proved a costly operation since two of a/c with complete crews are 'Missing' and another crashed after its crew had baled out safely in England'. One of the Wellingtons 'missing' was that flown by pilot Donald MacFarlane, with air gunner William Tyler, observer Alan Harvey, wireless operator/air gunner Malcolm Jones, and Canadian wireless operator/air gunner John Cormack.

Information slowly started to come through from German sources. Noting that the Wellington crashed in Bruehl, Kaiserstrasse at 0233 hours on 15 April, the Germans originally believed it was a crew of six and the remains were placed in six coffins and buried in Cologne South Cemetery.[81] Post-war exhumations revealed that identity of two of the crew, Alan Harvey and Malcolm Jones, and in one of the six graves there were no remains left except for pieces of a Mae West. In moving the crew to Rheinberg Cemetery Harvey and Jones were given their own graves and William, Donald MacFarlane and John Cormack were laid to rest in a collective grave.

ALSO HIS WIFE LILIAN, CHILDREN BRIAN AND NOVA KILLED BY ENEMY ACTION. THEY LIVE WITH US IN MEMORY STILL

AIRCRAFTMAN 2ND CLASS ROYAL POTTER
GROUND STAFF (RAFVR), NO. 150 SQUADRON
DIED 27TH APRIL 1942, AGED 27
BURIED NORWICH CEMETERY, UNITED KINGDOM

At this stage of the war, the controversial area bombing offensive against German cities, designed to 'de-house' civilians working in war production roles, was beginning to be effective enough for the German authorities to plan a tit-for-tat retaliation.

During April and May 1942, they carried out a series of similar attacks on British towns and cities, chosen entirely for their cultural and historic significance rather than for any military objectives. They became known as the Baedeker Blitz, after the German language tourist guidebook that was used to select the targets.

Following on from the devastating London Blitz, German expectations were high but the British defences were better than they had anticipated, partly due to the introduction of onboard night fighter radar, resulting in unsustainably high Luftwaffe bomber losses. Nevertheless, the attacks on Bath, Canterbury, Exeter, Norwich and York resulted in countless damaged or destroyed homes and more than 1,500 civilian deaths.

Royal Potter was a member of the ground staff at No. 150 Squadron, RAF Snaith. He was at home on leave with his wife and two children at No. 6, St. Mary's Road, Norwich on the night of 27 April when the Germans attacked the city. His son Brian Royal Potter was ten years of age and Nova, his daughter, was just three. St. Mary's Road took a direct hit from a 1000kg 'Hermann' bomb, which was designed for demolition. Several streets in the area were reduced to rubble and what few homes remained were fit only for razing to the ground.

The Potters were not the only family to perish in this attack. Hilda Lockwood of Roseberry Road and her three children, one just three months old; Maud Miller and her two daughters, to name but a few. Twenty-three of more than 200 deaths were children under sixteen.

Unlike Royal Potter, the fathers of most of the children were spared, probably because they were away on war service. It is difficult to imagine what it would have been like for them to receive such dreadful news, possibly while overseas.[82]

NOT ALL THE DARKNESS IN THE WORLD
CAN DIM THE LIGHT OF ONE SMALL CANDLE

PILOT OFFICER LESLIE NEWTON
OBSERVER (RAFVR), NO. 156 SQUADRON
DIED 30TH MAY 1942, AGED 31
BURIED BERGEN-OP-ZOOM WAR CEMETERY, NETHERLANDS

The epitaph chosen is a slight adaptation of a quote by St. Francis of Assisi, which is generally taken to read, 'All the darkness in the world cannot extinguish the light of a single candle.' The context and the changes make it very personal to Leslie's family. The word 'extinguish' is so final, and perhaps replacing it with 'dim' suggests a fuller defiance of the darkness surrounding Leslie's loss – the memory of the Newton family's 'one small candle' will not fade.

The night of 30/31 May 1942 was one of the major turning points of the air war, the first thousand bomber raid. With the help of crews from training units, Bomber Command sent over a thousand aircraft to attack Cologne. Having taken off at 2315 hours from RAF Alconbury Leslie Newton's No. 156 Squadron Wellington was one of forty-one aircraft that failed to return, shot down by a night fighter.

In September 1945 an officer from No. 5 Holland Section of the Missing Research and Enquiry Service, visited the crash site at Tholen.[83]

> I was informed by a Secretary of the Town Hall of Tholen … that an aircraft believed to be a Wellington bomber, crashed 3 kms. south of Tholen, in May, 1942, during the return journey from what was believed to be the first 1000 bomber raid on Cologne. (This was heard on the B.B.C. news).
> It was further learnt that a Mr J. Schot … at present with the Royal Netherlands Navy in Skegness, England, assisted in transporting the bodies of the crew to Bergen op Zoom. I went to see Mrs Schott who produced the undermentioned effects.
> One leather wallet containing a Registration Card and photograph belonging to W.T. Cormack [the pilot].
> The Burgomaster of Bergen op Zoom confirmed the above facts and from records held by him, it was revealed that the crew were killed on 31st May. 1942, but no burial dates were available.
> The crew are buried in the German Cemetery, Wouwsche Straatweg, Bergen op Zoom … which are kept in good order and bear simple wooden crosses.

The two Canadian members of the crew were reburied in Bergen-op-Zoom Canadian Cemetery, whilst Leslie and his three other crewmates were buried in the adjacent Bergen-op-Zoom War Cemetery.

BACK TO THE COINER THE MINTAGE OF MAN – LADS WHO DIED IN GLORY TO NEVER GROW OLD

SERGEANT MICHAEL BRUCE ROGERSON
PILOT (RAFVR), NO. 103 SQUADRON
DIED 31ST MAY 1942, AGED 20
BURIED REICHSWALD FOREST WAR CEMETERY, GERMANY

An excerpt from an 1896 poem entitled *The Lads in Their Hundreds* by Alfred Edward Housman and written about the Second Boer War but which became popular in the First World War. Surprisingly perhaps, it only features in three Bomber Command epitaphs. It and several other works by Housman were later set to music by Lieutenant George Butterworth MC MiD of the Durham Light Infantry, who was himself killed in action on 5 August 1916 during the Battle of the Somme. The full poem reads:

> The lads in their hundreds to Ludlow come in for the fair,
> There's men from the barn and the forge and the mill and the fold,
> The lads for the girls and the lads for the liquor are there,
> And there with the rest are the lads that will never be old.
>
> There's chaps from the town and the field and the till and the cart,
> And many to count are the stalwart, and many the brave,
> And many the handsome of face and the handsome of heart,
> And few that will carry their looks or their truth to the grave.
>
> I wish one could know them, I wish there were tokens to tell
> The fortunate fellows that now you can never discern;
> And then one could talk with them friendly and wish them farewell
> And watch them depart on the way that they will not return.
>
> But now you may stare as you like and there's nothing to scan;
> And brushing your elbow unguessed-at and not to be told
> They carry back bright to the coiner the mintage of man,
> The lads that will die in their glory and never be old.[84]

The coiner in this context is God and the penultimate line of the poem metaphorically laments how the newly minted coins (the Lads) will return to their maker all too soon, while still bright and untarnished.

Michael Rogerson's flying career was indeed all too short, comprising only two operational sorties: St. Nazaire and Köln.[85] The latter was the first of the 'Thousand Bomber Raids', and arguably the most successful. Nothing was heard from the aircraft after leaving RAF Elsham Wolds in what is now North Lincolnshire. All six airmen perished and were initially laid to rest in Waltrop Municipal Cemetery but later 'concentrated' to Reichswald.[86]

DID WE DO WELL? WE DIED AND NEVER KNEW
BUT WELL OR ILL ENGLAND, WE DIED FOR YOU

SERGEANT STANLEY DENNIS ENGLAND
WIRELESS OPERATOR/AIR GUNNER (RAFVR), NO. 149 (EAST INDIA) SQUADRON
DIED 6TH JUNE 1942, AGED 25
BURIED REICHSWALD FOREST WAR CEMETERY, GERMANY

Numerous military epitaphs are attributed to the English classicist and poet John Maxwell Edmonds. On 6 February 1918 *The Mail*[87] featured a piece by Edmonds titled 'Four Epitaphs' The second of these, titled, 'On Some who died early in the Day of Battle', reads

> Went the day well? we died and never knew;
> But well or ill, England, we died for you.

Since publication Edmonds' epitaphs have been widely used both in official publications, on war memorials and at commemorations, and on personal headstones. The relatives of eleven Bomber Command fatalities used the 'Went the day well?' epitaph as the basis for their inscriptions. Some replaced 'England' with 'Freedom'. The family of Stanley Mitchell, killed on 30 October 1939, made it very personal to their son with 'I died for you', and the family of David Lock, killed on 4 July 1943, chose 'he died for you'. For Stanley England, the son of Charles and Louisa, from Southend-On-Sea, and husband to Olive, the choice of opening words for the inscription is the only one of the eleven that further adapts Edmonds' epitaph, choosing 'Did we do well?'

On the night of 5/6 June 1942 Stanley's Short Stirling took off from RAF Lakenheath at 2322 hours detailed for a raid on Essen. Shot down near Duisberg-Wannheimerort, Germany, there was a total loss of life and the crew of seven, who were originally buried in Düsseldorf North Cemetery, were reburied in the Reichswald Forest War Cemetery in December 1946.

One of the difficulties faced by those left behind, when an airman was reported missing, is revealed in a letter from the Glasspool Charity Trust to the Air Ministry, dated 17 November 1942 just over 5 months after Stanley had been reported missing.[88]

> The attention of my Trust has been drawn to the wife of [Stanley England] who is expecting a child at any moment. She was a WAAF until April when she left the service and is now in receipt of a pension of £1.0s.6d. She is in a rather difficult position as there is no certainty regarding her husband's death and in view of this she has to pay premiums on her husband's Insurances amounting to the sum of £1.13.9.d per month. This is of course an impossibility for her to do, without neglecting herself and I am wondering whether it is possible for a temporary certificate of death to be issued in order that she may be relieved of this great expense.

A notification was issued by the Air Ministry on 9 December certifying that it was now 'presumed, for official purposes', that Stanley had lost his life.

DEMOCRACY, THAT IS SO WELL WORTH DYING FOR, MUST BE MADE WORTH LIVING FOR

FLIGHT SERGEANT WILLIAM EDGAR PILBOROUGH
WIRELESS OPERATOR/AIR GUNNER (RCAF), NO. 35 (MADRAS PRESIDENCY) SQUADRON
DIED 8TH JUNE 1942, AGED 30
BURIED HEVERLEE WAR CEMETERY, BELGIUM

William's family chose to appeal to the epitaph reader, to place great value on the sacrifice they made in the name of democracy. And that this must not be taken for granted. Those left behind have a duty to honour that sacrifice and continue to advance and progress democratic ideals.

Born on 11 August 1915, the son of William and Gertrude J. Pilborough, of Chateauquay Basin, Canada, and having shown a keen interest in sport at school, William became a sports writer and layout editor on a newspaper in Montreal prior to enlistment on 13 September 1940. In his interview for the RCAF Special Reserve the interviewer noted William as 'Good type, keen, courteous, steady nerves, bright.' And later the Chief Instructor of No. 7 Bombing and Gunnery School would record him as 'Above average. Hard working and intelligent.'[89]

Passing through No. 19 Operational Training Unit and then No. 1652 Conversion Unit, William arrived at No. 35 (Madras Presidency) Squadron, based at RAF Linton-on-Ouse. On the night of 22/23 May 1942, as the wireless operator on Sergeant Pack's crew, William's aircraft took off at 23.53 hours detailed to raid St Nazaire, but poor weather frustrated their attack, and the bombs were jettisoned in the sea.

Their next raid was more successful, as part of the first Thousand Bomber raid, their post raid report recording 'Bright moonlight, visibility excellent. Bombs dropped one mile south of aiming point, bursts not observed through fires.' Raids to Essen (2/3 June) and Bremen (3/4 June) followed, although William doesn't appear in the crew list for Sergeant Pack when attacking Emden on 6/7 June. On the 8 June William's crew was one of ten detailed at No. 35 Squadron, to attack Essen. Only six returned, reporting searchlights and intense anti-aircraft over the target. Flak damage had forced one aircraft to ditch in the North Sea, but against the other crews the Operations Record Book recorded 'Nothing was heard of this aircraft after leaving base.'[90]

William is buried with four of his crew in a collective grave at Heverlee War Cemetery, Belgium.

A PAGE IN MY BOOK OF MEMORIES IS GENTLY TURNED TODAY. NORMAN JR.

FLIGHT SERGEANT ERNEST NORMAN JEFFERIES
AIR GUNNER (RCAF), NO. 405 (VANCOUVER) SQUADRON
DIED 9TH JUNE 1942, AGED 29
BURIED RHEINBERG WAR CEMETERY, GERMANY

Ernest was born 17 May 1913 in the Côte-des-Neiges neighbourhood of Montreal. His father Walter was a British immigrant who had seen action in the First World War. Ernest had been working as a bookkeeper before enlisting on 27 March 1940. After initial training in Canada, he was posted overseas the following January, and on arrival in England underwent further training at several units before becoming operational at No. 405 Squadron, RAF Pocklington, on 28 October 1941.[91]

Between enlisting and being called for duty, he had married Ruby Carson, also of Montreal, where they had set up a home together.[92]

His first operational sortie on the night of 6/7 January 1942 was a bombing attack on the Cherbourg docks through 'lucky cloud breaks'. The attack was considered relatively low risk because little flying over occupied territory was required, as a result of which the squadron sent five 'fresher' crews.

Thirteen further successful operations ensued between then and the first week in June but on 8/9 June the squadron was tasked with bombing Essen in the Ruhr Valley – or 'Happy Valley' as crews had ironically christened it. It was home to the mighty Krupps steel foundries and armament factories and, being within easy reach of England, was defended accordingly. It wasn't Ernest's first trip to Essen and having attacked it back in March, April and just a week earlier on 1 June, he would certainly have known what a formidable target it could be.

No. 405 detailed eleven Halifax aircraft to fly that night, although one failed to take off due to technical problems. Of the remaining ten, three failed to return, including Ernest's, which was coned by searchlights and hit by heavy flak. All but the flight engineer, Sergeant Derek Riches, were killed and initially laid to rest in the British military cemetery at Köln-Zolstock before being moved to Rheinberg in summer 1946. Riches was incarcerated for the remainder of the war in numerous Stalag Luft camps.[93]

Back home in Canada, Ruby was expecting their first child: a son that Norman Sr. was never to meet. Ernest Norman Jr. was born 28 October 1941, the very day that Norman became operational. Although Norman Jr. could not have penned the words of the epitaph himself, perhaps it provided some comfort as he grew up and came to understand the sacrifice that his father and so many others had made.[94]

"THE LAST SCORER WILL WRITE THAT YOU PLAYED THE GAME"

SERGEANT NIEL MALCOLM HARDY
AIR GUNNER (RAAF), NO. 50 SQUADRON
DIED 26TH JUNE 1942, AGED 20
BURIED BECKLINGEN WAR CEMETERY, GERMANY

(Many of the official records and websites show the spelling of Sergeant Hardy's first name as 'Neil'. The handwritten parts of his service record show Niel.)

Niel's personal records show that he, a resident of Toowoomba, Australia, enlisted at No. 3 Recruiting Centre, Brisbane, on 6 December 1940, the day after his nineteenth birthday. On his 'Application for Air Crew' form submitted earlier in the year Niel mentioned his previous sporting achievements, having played in the 1st XI cricket and 1st XV football teams at school. Owing to the fact Niel is under the age of twenty-one his application is signed by his mother Olive, her son's sporting prowess referenced in the choice of epitaph. Indeed, sporting references appear on many Australian aircrew epitaphs.

American sports journalist Grantland Rice achieved notoriety in the first half of the twentieth century with his insightful and clever prose both as a sportswriter and as a poet and author. For Niel's epitaph his family drew upon Rice's quote, 'For when the One Great Scorer comes to write against your name, He marks - not that you won or lost - but how you played the game', clearly wishing their son to be remembered as a young man of good conduct, character, and integrity.

Niel embarked for Canada from Sydney in January 1941, subsequently sailing to the UK in September that year. Via No. 1 Signals School and No. 14 Operational Training Unit, Niel arrived at No. 50 Squadron in June 1942. His personal records show that he trained as a wireless operator/air gunner, although on the fateful night a colleague is listed as the wireless operator on their Manchester, with Niel carrying out air gunner duties. This was Niel's first operation with No. 50 Squadron.

The attack on Bremen on the night of 25/26 June 1942 was planned as another thousand bomber raid, with No. 50 Squadron contributing 14 Manchesters to the attacking force. Niel's aircraft left the RAF Swinderby runway at 2320 hours but, as the squadron diary would state, 'Nothing heard of this aircraft after airbourne', and the crew were classified as 'Missing'. Eventually the Air Ministry received a telegram from the International Red Cross, 'quoting Berlin information' stating that the entire crew were 'all dead'. As such Niel and his colleagues were now classified 'Missing believed Killed in Action'. In January 1947 Niel, having previously been buried in Bremen-Walle Cemetery, was reinterred at Becklingen War Cemetery. One other member of his crew has their own grave. The five others share a collective grave with two members of a No. 15 Operational Training Unit Wellington shot down on the same night.

GOODBYE, DADDY. MICHAEL AND GEORGINA

SQUADRON LEADER GEORGE WILLIAM ALEXANDER
PILOT (RAFVR), NO. 149 (EAST INDIA) SQUADRON
DIED 29TH JUNE 1942, AGED 38
BURIED WONSERADEEL (MAKKUM) PROTESTANT CHURCHYARD, NETHERLANDS

George had originally served in No. 1503 Beam Approach Training Flight and was posted to No. 149 Squadron on 23 June 1942.[95] Just two days later he flew as 'second dickie' to captain Flight Lieutenant William Barnes DFC aboard a Short Stirling, the very first four-engine heavy bomber to enter service. Barnes was an RAF regular with much experience and had at one point been temporary Officer Commanding of No. 149 Squadron Conversion Flight.

Their target for the night was Bremen and it was possible for the crew to see their own bomb bursts through the thin cloud that prevailed over the target that night. A four hour round trip and back in time for debrief before a bacon and 'real eggs' breakfast – something enjoyed only by aircrew returning from a night-time operation.

Four days later still he flew his second and last operation, again to Bremen, to attack the Focke-Wulf aircraft factory and AG Weser U-boat shipyard, and once again with Flight Lieutenant Barnes as captain. The take-off time was similar and it should have been a carbon copy of his first sortie.

Sadly though, it was anything but. Damaged by flak over the target, their aircraft was then shot down by a night fighter flown by Leutnant Hans-Georg Bötel of 6./NJG 2, crashing close to Bolsward in the Netherlands.[96] Of the eight airmen on board, seven, including George, perished in the crash. Only one of the wireless operator/air gunners, Australian Sergeant Leonard Collins, was able to bail out. He landed safely and was given a hot meal by a local family before being captured. He spent most of the war incarcerated in Stalag Luft VIII-B, Lamsdorf.[97] Those who died were laid to rest in a collective grave in Makkum Cemetery.

It is often thought that airmen of Bomber Command were young, single men. Young they certainly were; their average age being just twenty-three. However, a considerable proportion – around a quarter – were married.[98]

At thirty-eight, George was much older than might be considered usual for Bomber Command aircrew although with an average age of twenty-eight, the same could be said of the majority of this crew. He was married to Dorothy and they had two children, Michael and Georgina.

REMEMBERING ALSO HIS WIFE MOIRA, LOST IN S.S. "CERAMIC" 6.12.42. AGE 22

FLIGHT SERGEANT NORMAN TETLEY
PILOT (RAFVR), NO. 44 (RHODESIA) SQUADRON
DIED IST AUGUST 1942, AGED 26
BURIED RHEINBERG WAR CEMETERY, GERMANY

No. 44 Squadron crews returning from the large and devastating raid to Düsseldorf on the night of 31 July/1 August reported, 'Town well ablaze', 'extremely large fires', 'billowing smoke covered most of the area'. They also reported on the heavy defences, 'We were approached by two Me110s', 'Flak was heavy', 'One aircraft was seen to be shot down', 'A lot of very good S/L [searchlight] cones holding aircraft and firing light flak straight up them'. In the squadron diary, against the crew of Norman Tetley, no such reports were made, the entry reading, 'Aircraft MISSING. No signals received'. There were no survivors from Norman's crew, his Lancaster one of twenty-nine aircraft lost that night. Having crashed near Mönchengladbach the crew were originally buried in the town cemetery, and then reburied in Rheinberg War Cemetery in July 1946.[99]

Norman's parents, Arthur and Ellen Tetley were from Durban, Natal, South Africa. They chose, for the epitaph, to also commemorate their son's wife, Moira, who has no grave and is recorded as having died at sea. Moira, whose parents came from Salisbury, Southern Rhodesia, and no doubt still grieving the recent loss of Norman, boarded the ocean liner *SS Ceramic* in Liverpool in November 1942, bound for Australia via Saint Helena and South Africa, and initially travelling in convoy. Moira is listed as a civilian passenger in the company of not just the crew but also military personnel, which included thirty nurses of the Queen Alexandra's Imperial Military Nursing Service, and twelve children.

On the night of 6/7 December the ship, now, as planned, separated from the convoy, was attacked by a German U-boat, and struck by three torpedoes. With the *Ceramic* severely damaged, the liner's 656 occupants took to the lifeboats, before another attack then sent the *Ceramic* to the bottom of the ocean. During the night, in a raging storm, many lifeboats capsized. The U-boat commander did return the next morning but only picked up one man. There were no other survivors.[100]

HERE PAT SLEEPS NEAR HIS CREW OF FOUR
IN HIS LITTLE BIT OF TEXAS FOR EVERMORE

FLIGHT SERGEANT PAT NEFF TEMPLETON
PILOT (RCAF), NO. 22 OPERATIONAL TRAINING UNIT
DIED 7TH SEPTEMBER 1942, AGED 19
BURIED BICESTER CEMETERY, UNITED KINGDOM

The all-RCAF crew aboard Wellington HF865 were on a routine night navigation exercise when they experienced a loss of power during a turn, resulting in a stall. The aircraft crashed near Bicester in Oxfordshire with the loss of all five airmen.

Pat, the captain, hailed from Wellington in the Texan 'pan-handle'. Yet he, like the rest of the crew, were enlisted in the Royal Canadian Air Force. The reasons for this may be identified by observing his date of enlistment: 14 April 1941. Before Pearl Harbor and American's subsequent entry into the war.

Pat had made a conscious decision to break the neutrality laws which existed in America at the time and make the long journey to Canada. In doing so he risked his own nationality, since he could easily have been refused entry back into America. In all probability he was responding to a call to enlist from the Clayton Knight Committee, set up by a Canadian First World War ace, Air Marshal Billy Bishop VC, and his American friend Clayton Knight. Its purpose was to address the serious shortfall in pilots that the British and Canadian air forces were experiencing by recruiting American commercial pilots and those with private pilot's licenses.

Recruitment took place in plain sight, despite the risks involved, often in prestigious hotels such as New York's *Waldorf Astoria*, although the situation had eased a little by the time of Pat's enlistment after the signing of the lease-lend agreement. In truth the American government, and Roosevelt in particular, were sympathetic to their cause and largely turned a blind eye.

Pat's Canadian attestation papers list thirty-six solo hours' flying. Surprisingly, he also signed the Oath to His Majesty the King, this being largely regarded as optional for non-Canadian citizens.[101]

Had he survived a while longer, he would have been given the opportunity to transfer to a unit within the 'Mighty Eighth' of the US Army Air Force, which had arrived in Great Britain a matter of three months before his death. Many did, subject to their commanding officer's release, whereas others chose to stay with their crew. Some were granted permission once their tour expired but were killed in the intervening time and are easily identified by having US service numbers while still in the RCAF.

Approximately 570 American aircrew were lost on the strength of RAF Bomber Command during the Second World War.[102] Many of these were Clayton Knight Committee recruits.

OH! FOR THE SOUND OF A VOICE THAT IS STILL

FLIGHT SERGEANT KEITH CAMPBELL BENNETT
AIR GUNNER (RAAF), NO. 460 (AUSTRALIAN) SQUADRON
DIED 14TH SEPTEMBER 1942, AGED 22
BURIED RHEINBERG WAR CEMETERY, GERMANY

Shortly after dropping their bombs on Düsseldorf in the early hours of 16 August 1942, the crew of Wellington UV-K, with Australian Keith Bennett in the rear turret, became aware of what appeared to be Junkers 88 approaching, about 200 yards distant and slightly above. The night fighter unleashed cannon and machine gun fire, which tore through the armour-plated doors and riddled the Wellington amidships. The wireless operator was hit in the thighs and the pilot sent his bomber into a steep dive. Keith Bennett, 'rotating his gun turret 45 degrees to port opened fire on the enemy aircraft which was 70-100 yards distant and slightly above. In all one burst of 6-7 seconds was fired and tracers were seen entering the enemy aircraft at the wing roots and front of the fuselage which went into a climbing turn to port. A yellowish green flame broke out at the root of the port wing and the aircraft stalled and fell away enveloped in flames and is claimed to have been destroyed... the Wellington sustained damage to fabric and geodetics. Some bullets entered at the rear end of the bomb bays and emerged through the front turret causing considerable damage to the wiring and putting the hydraulic system out of action so that the emergency system had to be used for lowering the undercarriage, it was also impossible to close the bomb doors.'[103]

For his actions that night the pilot was awarded the Distinguished Flying Medal, news of which was published just days before his and Keith's final flight on the night of 13/14 September, on which there was a total loss of life.

The epitaph chosen is a slightly adapted quote from the poem *Break, Break, Break* by Alfred, Lord Tennyson, an elegy expressing a longing for a lost friend. Life goes on around him, but the feeling of loss remains.

(Third stanza)
And the stately ships go on
To their haven under the hill;
But O for the touch of a vanish'd hand,
And the sound of a voice that is still!

IL VECUT CE QUE VIVENT LES ROSES, L'ESPACE D'UN MATIN

SERGEANT RENÉ LAUGHTON PARTINGTON
AIR GUNNER (RAFVR), NO. 142 SQUADRON
DIED 6TH OCTOBER 1942, AGED 21
BURIED CAMBRIDGE CITY CEMETERY, UNITED KINGDOM

&

SERGEANT JOHN CLAUDE PARTINGTON
PILOT (RAFVR), NO. 9 (IX) SQUADRON
DIED 9TH JUNE 1941, AGED 20.
BURIED FLUSHING (VLISSINGEN) NORTHERN CEMETERY, NETHERLANDS.

Translation from French
HE LIVED AS LONG AS ROSES LIVE, THE SPAN OF A MORNING

John and René were both born in Argentina, although their family hailed from Worcestershire. Their father John Laughton Partington, who was already living in Argentina at the outbreak of the First World War, served as a major in the Royal Engineers and had been awarded the Military Cross for his prompt action and courage in arranging an evacuation of trucks and ammunition while under intense shell fire.[104] He had also been Mentioned in Despatches.[105] Less than a year after returning to Buenos Aires from Falmouth, he married Madelaine Pleasance, whose parents were French and German. He worked as an engineer at Saxby & Farmer, railway signalling equipment manufacturers, and was a cricketer of some repute. The couple had two sons – René and John – both of whom were educated at Cheltenham College in England.

Both sons volunteered for the RAF Volunteer Reserve; John had just completed his second year reading engineering at Trinity Hall, Cambridge University when he enlisted.[106] He first flew operationally as second pilot on the night of 7/8 June 1941, attacking the German cruiser *Prinz Eugen* at Brest. The next day, the same crew were detailed aboard the same aircraft for a daylight attack on enemy shipping off the Belgian and Dutch coast.[107] Intercepted off Zeebrugge and shot down into the sea, only the rear gunner survived.

René, an air gunner with No. 142 Squadron, at RAF Grimsby, arrived on 3 May 1942 from No. 23 OTU. His first operational sortie was on 30 May against Köln. He took part in twenty-five further successful operations, but on the night of 5/6 October his aircraft crashed near Princetown in Devon returning from an attack on Aachen.[108] How the aircraft became so seriously off course is a mystery, although visibility was extremely poor. Why René was buried at Cambridge is unknown, since unlike John, he had not studied there, although connections with the area existed owing to his mother having studied there. Both headstones are engraved with the same epitaph, taken from a poem by 16th century French poet François de Malherbe and no doubt influenced by their mother's French roots.

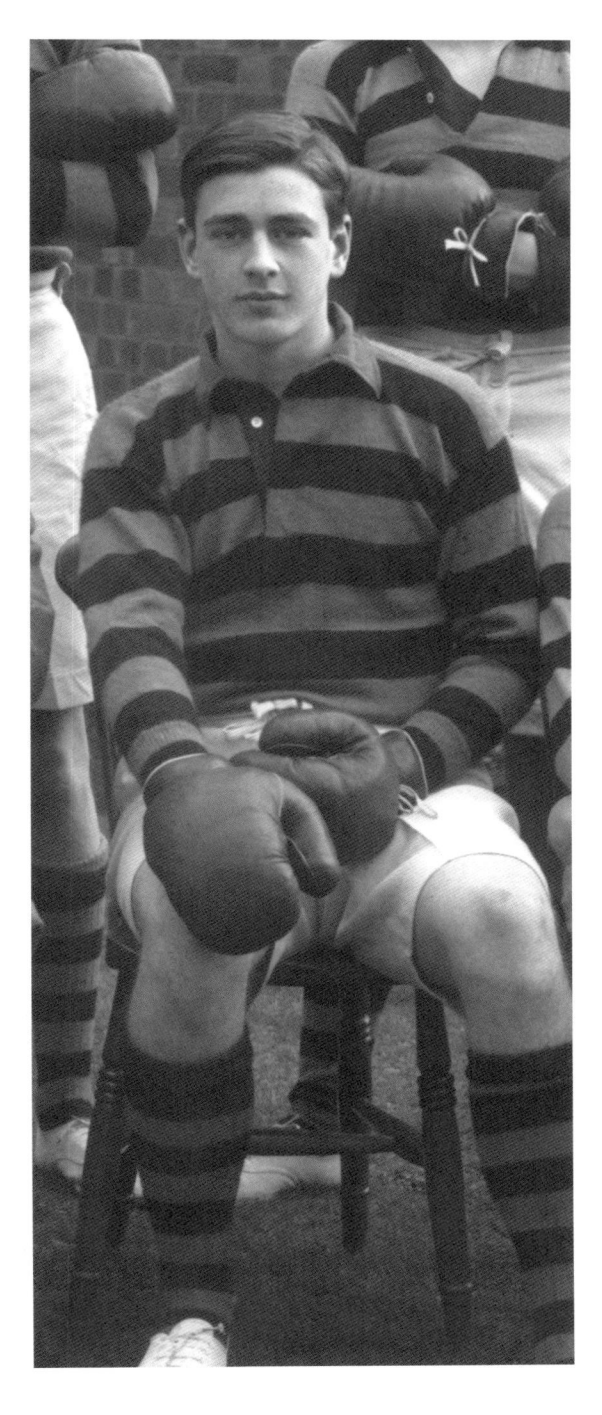

John Claude Partington at Cheltenham College.

PER ARDUA AD ASTRA
966815 WARRANT OFFICER
D. A. GEE
PILOT
ROYAL AIR FORCE
7TH OCTOBER 1942 AGE 22
WE ALL THANK YOU TONY.
YOUR WIFE IRENE AND PARENTS
"A GOOD FRIEND
AND A GRAND CAPTAIN"
YOUR CREW

WE ALL THANK YOU TONY. YOUR WIFE IRENE AND PARENTS. "A GOOD FRIEND AND A GRAND CAPTAIN" YOUR CREW

WARRANT OFFICER DONALD ANTHONY GEE
PILOT (RAFVR), NO. 28 OPERATIONAL TRAINING UNIT
DIED 7TH OCTOBER 1942, AGED 22
BURIED BURTON-ON-THE-WOLDS BURIAL GROUND, UNITED KINGDOM

More than eight thousand losses were sustained by Bomber Command just in training during the Second World War.[109] Only a small fraction of those were truly operational, as it was normal practice for crews nearing graduation to fly one or two relatively 'safe' operations, such as 'Nickel' raids (dropping propaganda leaflets) over France, or occasionally minelaying. The notable occasion during which trainee crews flew over the Reich was during the 'Thousand Bomber Raids' when Sir Arthur Harris, Air Officer Commanding-in-Chief RAF Bomber Command, called upon every airworthy aircraft he could lay his hands on, just to make up the numbers. Unsurprisingly perhaps, many of these inexperienced crews were lost during those three attacks.

Donald Gee was born in Spring 1920 in Hutton, Lancashire to Leslie and Delphine Gee. He married Irene Sadler in the second quarter of 1942 in Preston[110], by which time he was nearing the end of his operational flying training. Based at RAF Wymeswold in Leicestershire, he and two other crew members (second pilot, Flight Sergeant Albert Barkel and wireless operator/air gunner, Flight Sergeant Leslie Jones) set out on a daylight training sortie using the dual controls fitted as standard on Wellington bombers. This was a smaller crew than would be considered normal for an operational sortie, which usually comprised five or six for a 'Wimpy', as this aircraft was affectionately known. Since this was specific training for the pilots in the local area, only the wireless operator was required in addition.

Shortly after 4pm the aircraft was seen to jettison fuel before crashing at Woodhouse Eaves, three miles south of Loughborough. The Wimpy, designed by legendary aircraft engineer Barnes Wallis, was famously constructed using an immensely strong Geodetic lattice framework simply covered with fabric, the latter being prone to damage or being burned away. The board of enquiry heard that the fabric covering a vital part of the starboard wing may have stripped away in flight, seriously affecting the aerodynamics of the aircraft and possibly causing the crash.

Two of the three airmen were returned to their hometowns for burial, whereas Donald was buried just a few short miles from the crash site.[111] His epitaph, which appears to have been jointly written by his family and surviving crew, some of whom were mercifully not on board that day, speaks from the heart of their gratitude not only for being a 'grand captain' but also for his friendship.

MOTHER, I'VE WEIGHED THE RISKS WHICH I PREFER TO LIVING IN A WORLD DOMINATED BY NAZIS. BILL.

SERGEANT WILLIAM THOMAS MCDONALD
AIR GUNNER (RAFVR), NO. 50 SQUADRON
DIED 25TH OCTOBER 1942, AGED 25
BURIED BROOKWOOD MILITARY CEMETERY, UNITED KINGDOM

Bill was born to Robert and Hannah McDonald, the second of five children. Robert, a shepherd, had emigrated to Argentina to manage a sheep farm and later moved to Punta Arenas, Chile, where Bill was born on 7 February 1917.[112]

After a period with No. 25 OTU, Bill was posted to No. 50 Squadron, RAF Skellingthorpe in Lincolnshire, and flew his first 'op' against Düsseldorf on 10 September aboard Lancaster R5733.

According to the Operations Records Books[113] he had flown at least eight operations by the time of his fateful trip in 1942, when the crew was tasked with a long and risky daylight attack to Milan along with eighty-seven other Lancasters. His skipper was Flight Lieutenant Abercromby and their aircraft was Avro Lancaster W4135. It was the first attack on the city since 1940 and came as a complete surprise to the residents.

On the outward journey, their aircraft was running well behind schedule and came under sustained heavy flak bombardment, probably as a result of being a 'straggler'. Abercromby dived down to treetop level to avoid the flak, only to be hit by machine gun fire from rooftop defences. McDonald was hit by the fire and the mid-upper gun turret was also put out of action.

Unable to get an accurate fix on their position, they bombed a target of opportunity – a large warehouse – after which the mid-upper gunner dragged Bill from his turret. The flight engineer tended his wounds while the gunner took Bill's place in the rear turret.

Abercromby landed at the first available opportunity (RAF Boscombe Down) in an effort to obtain urgent medical attention for Bill. He was rushed to Salisbury Hospital, but sadly died of his injuries the following day. The aircraft had sustained numerous bullet holes, the starboard inner engine hit, and the tailplane main spar damaged. Remarkably, none of the other crew members were injured.

Bill was laid to rest at the age of twenty-five in Brookwood Military Cemetery in Surrey and his parents used this chilling line from his last letter as his epitaph.

A GREAT SURFMAN FROM BYRON BAY, AUSTRALIA'S EASTERLY POINT

FLIGHT SERGEANT JOHN GLEN DENING
PILOT (RAAF), NO. 44 (RHODESIA) SQUADRON
DIED 17TH DECEMBER 1942, AGED 27
BURIED JONKERBOS WAR CEMETERY, NETHERLANDS

An audit clerk from Byron Bay, John was perhaps more interested in outdoor pursuits when he wasn't working, judging by his epitaph. His father's given names were Sportsman John.

Born 23 March 1915 in Oakland, New South Wales, he enlisted on 26 April 1941 and embarked for training in Canada in October, finally arriving in the UK in March 1942. By the time he had passed through No. 15 Operational Training Unit and No. 1661 Conversion Flight, it was November 1942 when he arrived at No. 44 Squadron[114], which was at that time based at RAF Waddington, close to the cathedral city of Lincoln.

A little over two weeks after he arrived he was to fly his first operation – a bombing attack on Nienburg, mid-way between Hanover and Bremen.[115] His machine was ED355, a Mk. I. Lancaster. No. 44 Squadron was the first to receive this renowned type and had only been operating them since March of the same year. An unusually small contingent of only seven aircraft were detailed for the attack.

He had not flown any second dickie ops as became standard practice later in the war and there was no safety in numbers on this very small raid. Unsurprisingly perhaps, this attack and similar ones flown by No. 5 Group that night were a costly failure.[116]

Of the seven aircraft tasked with Nienburg, three did not return, including John Dening's. Fifteen of the twenty-one aircrew died whereas six survived and were incarcerated in various prisoner of war camps. John and all his crew perished when they were intercepted and shot down by a night fighter flown by Hauptmann Helmut Lent of Stab. IV./NJG1[117], crashing onto a road between Waterloo & Harich in the Netherlands. All except the navigator, Pilot Officer Nias, who had arrived at No. 44 a month earlier, were on their maiden flight.

Bomber Command would not attack Nienburg again until March 1945 when the famous No. 617 'Dambusters' Squadron successfully attacked and destroyed the bridge over the River Weser, in part using 22,000 lb. Grand Slam bombs.

ED355 was unearthed during road construction work in 1951 and a stone memorial erected nearby.[118] The name of a local resistance fighter, Jacob Corn Nagelhout, was also added to the memorial.

"RESTING WHERE NO SHADOWS FALL"
EVER REMEMBERED BY WIFE AND FOUR LITTLE ONES

SERGEANT THOMAS WALKER
WIRELESS OPERATOR/AIR GUNNER (RAFVR), NO. 14 OTU
DIED 17TH FEBRUARY 1943, AGED 30
BURIED CARLISLE (DALSTON ROAD) CEMETERY, UNITED KINGDOM

At thirty years of age Thomas, formerly a builder's labourer, was well above the average age of Bomber Command airmen. Married to Irene (née Woodall), she and his parents John and Isabella must have drawn from this well-known four-line funeral verse when choosing his epitaph:

> Resting where no shadows fall
> In peaceful sleep he awaits us all;
> God will link the broken chain,
> When one by one we meet again.

The line in question features on some seventy-seven Bomber Command headstones[119] and has also been used extensively as the title of books, films and songs. The last two lines appear on a further thirteen inscriptions. Despite its widespread use, the verse is of unknown authorship.

On 17 February 1943, Thomas and four of his fellow trainees took off at 0420 hours from RAF Saltby, a satellite to No. 14 OTU's main station of RAF Cottesmore, for a night training exercise. During the flight, a fire broke out and the bomber was totally destroyed. Eye-witnesses stated that the bomber appeared to bank steeply after overshooting and then stalled from a height of around 800 feet before crashing close to Sproxton, mid-way between Grantham and Melton Mowbray. The air gunner Sergeant Woods survived, albeit with severe leg injuries.

The bodies of the airmen who perished were returned to their hometowns for burial, in Thomas' case to Denton Holme, Carlisle in the former county of Cumberland. Irene remarried in 1946 to Joseph Elliott and died in 1988, still resident in Carlisle.

The children referred to in the epitaph were Raymond, born in the second quarter of 1936, Doreen (second quarter, 1938), Anne (first quarter, 1940) and lastly Thomas junior born a year before his father's death.[120]

(Thomas' age is shown as thirty-two on the Commonwealth War Graves Commission website but the IBCC Losses database notes a birth date of 7 December 1912, aging Thomas as thirty at the time of his death.)

OF BARBADOS, B.W.I. IN LOVING MEMORY OF AN ONLY SON,
AN ONLY BROTHER. A LOSS WE'LL NEVER RECOVER

SERGEANT GREY DOYLE CUMBERBATCH
AIR BOMBER (RAFVR), NO. 100 SQUADRON
DIED 5TH MARCH 1943, AGED 21
BURIED LONG BENNINGTON (ST. SWITHUN) CHURCHYARD, UNITED KINGDOM

In 2008 the Barbados Postal Service issued commemorative stamps, one of which showed 'The Barbados Second Contingent', a group of twelve men recruited to serve with the Royal Air Force in the Second World War. One of those was Grey Cumberbatch, the son of Charles and Octavia Cumberbatch from St. Michael, Barbados, who not only travelled to the United Kingdom aboard the *SS Maaskerk* in November 1940, but also put his musical talents to good use entertaining the ship's company every evening on the piano.

Grey's Lancaster took off from RAF Grimsby at 1832 hours on the evening of 5 March 1943, detailed for a minelaying operation, but fog forced a diversion to RAF Langar on their return. Grey's Lancaster crashed while trying to land and the young Barbadian lost his life, with only one survivor from the crew of seven, the mid upper gunner. In 2012 a memorial was unveiled to the crew in Plungar, and Grey's sister visited her brother's grave in Long Bennington to place flowers.[121] Of the twelve men who formed 'The Barbados Second Contingent', six men, including Grey, would lose their lives.

Sergeant Charles Parnell King. Killed in a No. 9 Squadron Lancaster on the night of 25/26 June 1943. Charles is buried in the Harderwijk General Cemetery in the Netherlands.

Sergeant Arthur Adolphus Walrond. Killed in a No. 15 Squadron Stirling on the night of 28/29 June 1943. Arthur rests in the Heverlee War Cemetery in Belgium.

Sergeant Mark Radford Cuke. Killed in a No. 51 Operational Training Unit Blenheim on 17 November 1941 and buried in Kempston Cemetery. Epitaph – IN FREEDOM'S FIGHT TO RESCUE RIGHT HE GAVE ALL

Flying Officer Andrew Peter Cathcart Dunlop. Killed in a No. 10 Operational Training Unit Whitley on 10 December 1942. Andrew is buried in Brookwood Military Cemetery. Epitaph – AND NOW FOR HIM THE GLORY OF THE DAY HATH RISEN IN FULLER GRACE

Pilot Officer Bruce F.H. Miller DFC. Killed in a No. 103 Squadron Lancaster on the night of 22/23 October 1943. Bruce rests in Hanover War Cemetery, Germany. Epitaph – GREATER LOVE HATH NO MAN THAN THIS, THAT A MAN LAY DOWN HIS LIFE FOR HIS FRIENDS

O RYFEL! CHWERW EI OFWY'N
RHOI'I FAEN MUD AR EIFION MWYN

FLYING OFFICER HENRY EIFION CLEMENT
NAVIGATOR (RAFVR), NO. 101 SQUADRON
DIED 15TH APRIL 1943, AGED 22
BURIED MAUBEUGE-CENTRE CEMETERY, FRANCE

Translation from Welsh
OH WAR! ITS BITTER VISITATION
SETS ITS SILENT STONE ON GENTLE EIFION

Henry, the son of William and Mary Clement, from Velindre, Swansea, was clearly known to his family by his middle name Eifion. In choosing the epitaph the family exclaim their despair of another 'bitter visitation', which took their son. A silent stone now marks the burial place of 'Gentle Eifion' in Maubeuge-Centre Cemetery, where he rests with his entire crew. Henry lies in row A. grave 20. In the same row, grave 15, rests a childhood friend of his from Swansea[122], Graham George Williams, who lost his life two days after Henry.

AT THE GOING DOWN OF THE SUN AND IN THE MORNING
WE WILL REMEMBER THEM

FLYING OFFICER GRAHAM GEORGE WILLIAMS
AIR GUNNER (RAFVR), NO. 102 (CEYLON) SQUADRON
DIED 17TH APRIL 1943, AGED 22
BURIED MAUBEUGE-CENTRE CEMETERY, FRANCE

Graham, the son of Alfred and Elizabeth Williams, of St Thomas, Swansea, was the holder of the George Medal. The following citation appeared in *The London Gazette* in January 1942.[123]

In June, 1941, ammunition in an aircraft exploded by spontaneous combustion. In spite of the explosions, Aircraftman Bland climbed on to the mainplane and unfastened the gun panels. By this time the ammunition tank was burning fiercely, so he released it from the gun. Leading Aircraftman Williams carried away the burning tank, which started to explode while he was carrying it. The presence of mind and courage shown by these two airmen undoubtedly saved the aircraft and probably the lives of the air crews and armourers who were emptying the remaining ammunition tanks.

WE MISS YOU AND WONDER WHY YOU WHO SO DESERVED TO LIVE, SO YOUNG SHOULD HAVE TO DIE

SERGEANT HOWARD BECK
AIR GUNNER (RAFVR), NO. 102 (CEYLON) SQUADRON
DIED 27TH APRIL 1943, AGED 21
BURIED TEXEL (DEN BURG) CEMETERY, NETHERLANDS

The crew training report from No. 1658 Conversion Unit noted that Howard was 'well disciplined and tidy' and as 'an ex-Armourer has a good knowledge of gunnery and turrets'.[124] In March 1943, along with his crew, he was posted to No. 102 Squadron RAF Pocklington. On 26 April the squadron detailed fourteen of their Halifaxes to take part in what became a 561 aircraft attack on Duisburg. Howard's all sergeant crew took off at 0041 hours the next day but failed to return. This would appear to be their first raid together, having not previously appeared in the squadron diary.[125]

In July news came through, via the International Red Cross, quoting German sources, that the bodies of Howard and two other members of the crew had been recovered near Texel Island, Holland, on 28 April. The bomb aimer on the crew was William Foley, and his local newspaper reported the loss, drawing upon the telegram to William's family, which no doubt used the same words as those sent to Howard's family. The paper recorded, 'Although there is, unhappily, little reason to doubt the accuracy of this report, the casualty will be recorded as 'missing believed killed,' until confirmed by further evidence, or until, in the absence of such evidence, it becomes necessary, owing to lapse of time to presume for official purposes that death has occurred.' This would, 'in the absence of confirmatory evidence' not be presumed until at least six months from the date at which the respective airman was reported missing.

It is presumed that the Halifax went down in the sea and the wireless operator and flight engineer, whose bodies remain missing, are commemorated on The Air Forces Memorial at Runnymede. Howard, William Foley and the navigator rest in Texel (Den Burg) Cemetery, Holland. The pilot lies in Vlieland General Cemetery, Holland and the other air gunner in Esbjerg (Fourfelt) Cemetery, Denmark.

HIS SUN WENT DOWN WHILE IT WAS YET DAY

FLIGHT SERGEANT JACK OLIPHANT WILSON
PILOT (RAAF), NO. 15 (XV) SQUADRON
DIED 26TH MAY 1943, AGED 21
BURIED JONKERBOS WAR CEMETERY, NETHERLANDS

This inscription is an adaptation of Jeremiah Chapter 15, Verse 9 of the Old Testament, yet it is only appropriate as an epitaph when considered out of context, since the whole verse reads:

> She who bore seven has grown feeble; she has fainted away; her sun went down while it was yet day; she has been shamed and disgraced. And the rest of them I will give to the sword before their enemies, declares the Lord.

Jack was born 18 October 1921, originally from Scone, New South Wales, but later of Bondi Bay on the southern flank of Sydney Harbour. He attended Randwick Intermediate High School followed by Sydney High School and then became a clerk at the Bank of New South Wales, studying economics part-time at the University of Sydney.

He enlisted on 16 August 1941 and after initial training left for Great Britain on 16 June the following year, becoming operational with No. 15 Squadron on 4 May 1943.[126]

Jack's first operation was as second dickie aboard Short Stirling BK611, which was made famous on 27 March 1943 when its crew, three of whom were New Zealanders, 'delivered' a 500 lb. bomb plastered with savings stamps attached by crowds in Trafalgar Square during 'Wings for Victory' week. The target for the special bomb was a factory in Berlin and it was released to a rousing chorus of 'Maori Battalion'. They had nicknamed the aircraft 'Te-Kooti' after the Māori warrior chief.[127]

On 4 May, Jack was fortunate enough to fly second dickie with this illustrious crew, which was to be the captain Irvine Renner's thirtieth and final trip before being 'screened' from operations.

Three operations later and once again in BK611, the aircraft succumbed to a mauling by flak over Düsseldorf, the target for the night, before finally crash-landing in a field close to Venlo.[128] One of the air gunners had bailed out in the confusion and the remaining three survivors evaded capture for a while before being apprehended: one in Brussels ten days later, then the other pair six weeks later in Paris.[129,130] The three who perished, including Jack, were initially buried in Venlo Military Cemetery.

"OURS NOT TO REASON WHY DARLING"
A WONDERFUL HUSBAND AND SON. TESS, MUM, DAD

FLYING OFFICER WALLACE CLIFFORD LUTHER
NAVIGATOR (RAFVR), NO. 158 SQUADRON
DIED 29TH MAY 1943, AGED 24
BURIED HEVERLEE WAR CEMETERY, BELGIUM

Wallace's 'MUM, DAD', Luke and Flora, came from St. Johns, Newfoundland, and 'TESS' refers to his wife Elspeth, from Oxford. The quote in the epitaph, perhaps referencing both heroism and tragedy, is an adaptation of a line from the poem *The Charge of the Light Brigade* written by Alfred, Lord Tennyson in December 1854. A few weeks previous, during the Battle of Balaclava in the Crimean War, the Light Brigade of the British cavalry, acting upon a misunderstood order, suffered extensive casualties making a frontal assault against Russian artillery, along what Tennyson would call the 'Valley of Death'.

> "Forward, the Light Brigade!"
> Was there a man dismayed?
> Not though the soldier knew
> Someone had blundered.
> Theirs not to make reply,
> Theirs not to reason why,
> Theirs but to do and die.
> Into the valley of Death
> Rode the six hundred.

During May 1943, as part of the Battle of the Ruhr, Wallace Luther and his crew attacked targets in what Bomber Command airmen would ironically call 'Happy Valley', owing to the heavy defences. Indeed, on the night of 27/28 May, as part of a force of 518 aircraft attacking Essen, the rudder controls on Wallace's Halifax were partially shattered by heavy flak and the port inner engine, fuselage and hydraulics damaged. Two nights later a large force of 719 Bomber Command aircraft carried out a devastating raid on Wuppertal. Thirty-three aircraft were lost, including Wallace's No. 158 Squadron Halifax, having taken off from RAF Lissett at 2213 hours, the squadron operations book recording, 'since when there has been no news of it.'[131] It is believed they were shot down by a German night fighter, with a total loss of life. At Heverlee War Cemetery Wallace has his own individual grave while his crewmates rest in a collective grave.

TO THE WORLD HE WAS BUT ONE,
TO US HE WAS THE WORLD

FLYING OFFICER EARLE STANLEY GARAI
AIR BOMBER (RAFVR), NO. 218 (GOLD COAST) SQUADRON
DIED 30TH MAY 1943, AGED 20
BURIED HOTTON WAR CEMETERY, BELGIUM

Surprisingly perhaps, this epitaph is attributed to the famous American children's author and cartoonist, Dr. Seuss. Theodor Seuss Geisel, to give him his real name, is undoubtedly better known for works such as *The Cat in the Hat* and *How the Grinch Stole Christmas*, these and other famous works having been penned after the war. Made popular by his whimsical, light-hearted style and quick meter, a quote such as the one used in this epitaph is not characteristic of his later works and one may be forgiven for not associating it with Seuss. Indeed, it cannot be found in any of his published books, nor is it known to whom he may have been referring, yet variations on it appear on no fewer than twenty-eight Bomber Command headstones.[132]

Earle Garai appears to have gone by his middle name while on squadron. Stationed at RAF Downham Market, he flew his first operation on 4 May 1943 against Dortmund.[133] Three weeks later, with five operations under his belt, his crew were detailed for an attack on Wuppertal as part of a 700-strong bomber stream. By this point in the war, Pathfinder target marking had become highly developed and on this occasion it was especially accurate, leading to what was probably the first instance of the devastating 'firestorm', which would later become synonymous with attacks on Hamburg and Dresden.

Earle and his crew were most likely shot down by a night fighter flown by Oberleutnant Heinz-Wolfgang Schnaufer of Stab. II./NJG1, although a flak battery also submitted a claim.[134] The aircraft came down close to Eupen in Belgium with the loss of all on board. Three, including Earle, were laid to rest in Hotton War Cemetery whereas the bodies of the other four were never found and so are commemorated on The Air Forces Memorial at Runnymede. Of the seven crew, one was Australian and two were New Zealanders.

Earle is also commemorated on a family grave in Surbiton Cemetery, London which speaks further of the family's anguish.

IN PROUD AND LOVING MEMORY OF OUR HAPPY BOY AND YOUNGEST
BROTHER F/O EARLE STANLEY GARAI, RAFVR. KILLED IN ACTION OVER
GERMANY 30TH MAY 1943 AGED 20 YEARS.

YOU LOVED LIFE BUT WEREN'T AFRAID TO DIE. TO GREATER SAFETY
THAN WE COULD PROVIDE YOU PROUDLY TURNED, AND FROM OUR
ARMS WITHDREW NOT KNOWING THAT UPON THE DAY YOU DIED,
DEATH CAME TO US OUR SON BUT NOT TO YOU.

LOVE DEEP AS THINE
LAYS HERE ITS BROKEN FLOWER

SQUADRON LEADER RONALD HUGH LAUD
PILOT (RAF), NO. 75 (NZ) SQUADRON
DIED 12TH JUNE 1943, AGED 27
BURIED HEVERLEE WAR CEMETERY, BELGIUM

New Zealander Ronald Laud joined the Royal Air Force prior to the outbreak of the Second World War. The New Zealand Government had chosen not to include epitaphs on the graves of their service personnel, but it seems that as Ronald is listed as serving with the RAF, it made him eligible. (In a Grave Concentration Report Form, in the column 'Regt. Or Corps the typed 'R.N.Z.A.F' is crossed out and 'RAF' written in red.)

On the respective raid to Düsseldorf Ronald and his Stirling crew fell victim to a night fighter in the early hours of 12 June 1943. Of the crew of eight only one man would survive. Initially buried in Brusthem (St. Trond) Cemetery all seven men were moved to Heverlee War Cemetery in February 1947.

We cannot be sure exactly who chose the epitaph as that record is not available, but it was probably Ronald's wife Doris. She has chosen a line from a poem *Epitaph, Over the grave of two brothers, A child and a youth*, written by English poet Felicia Hemans (1973–1835), which was published in *Hymns for Childhood* in 1834. The full poem reads.

Thou, that canst gaze upon thine own fair boy,
And hear his prayer's low murmur at thy knee,
And o'er his slumber bend in breathless joy,
Come to this tomb! it hath a voice for thee!
Pray!—thou art blest—ask strength for sorrow's hour,
Love, deep as thine, lays here its broken flower.

Thou that art gathering from the smile of youth,
Thy thousand hopes—rejoicing to behold
All the heart's depths before thee bright with truth,
All the mind's treasure silently unfold;
Look on this tomb!—for thee, too, speaks the grave,
Where God hath seal'd the fount of hope he gave.

All those whose sons and husbands returned from the war, 'canst gaze upon thine own fair boy', but for Doris her deep love was now a broken flower.

KAEMP FOR ALT, HVAD DU HAR KAERT, DO, OM SAA DET GAELDER!

FLYING OFFICER ARNE RHOAR HELVARD
PILOT (RAFVR), NO. 218 (GOLD COAST) SQUADRON
DIED 22ND JUNE 1943, AGED 28
BURIED LANGDORP CHURCHYARD, BELGIUM.

Translation from Danish
LIVE AND DIE FOR WHAT YOU LOVE. CHERISH AND DEFEND IT!

Arne Helvard was born on 10 March 1915 in Fredericia, Denmark, the son of telegraphist Jens and Angla. The family later lived in Hobro and Hadsund, where his father became a postmaster. Arne graduated from Randers Statsskole in 1933 and went on to Copenhagen Polytechnic to study civil engineering, but he didn't find it interesting so dropped out and instead joined the Naval Air Service. He received his wings at the end of 1936 and was promoted to Flyverløjtnant I (Flying Officer) in January 1939.[135]

Shortly after the declaration of war, and before Denmark was under German occupation, Arne was on a routine patrol off the Danish coast in a floatplane when a German vessel hit a mine. Most of the men aboard drowned but one was able to swim ashore, while another four clambered onto some wooden flotsam and were spotted by Arne's Observer. Despite the rough conditions, they landed alongside the raft and rescued the four Germans for which they were awarded the Fortjenstmedaljen i Sølv (Danish King's Medal of Merit) and a while later the Rettungsmedaille am Bande (German Rescue Medal).

He was demobilised following the German invasion and found some temporary work at commercial airports, but a friend he'd met at Polytechnic who had been working as a spy was recruited by MI6 and persuaded Arne to escape to England with him. They met with difficulties at every juncture and were arrested both by Swedish and British authorities along the way.

Arne was finally released in July 1942. He immediately volunteered for the RAF eventually being posted to No. 218 Squadron on 13 June 1943. Just eight days later he was to fly his first, and as it turned out, his last operational sortie, to Krefeld.

In what must be regarded as a cruel irony, having been decorated for saving four German servicemen, he and his crew were shot down by one. Oberleutnant Heinz-Wolfgang Schnaufer of Stab I./NJG1[136] was already an ace with twelve victories and would go on to survive the war as the most successful night fighter pilot in history with an astonishing 121 victories to his name. However, the ironies don't end there: having survived the war, Schnaufer was seriously injured in a road traffic accident in 1950 and died two days later.[137]

Arne's epitaph is taken from a Danish hymn which is often used at funerals.

"YOUR MEMORY HALLOWED IN THE LAND YOU LOVED"

WARRANT OFFICER CLASS II RICHARD DOUGLAS TOD
AIR GUNNER (RCAF), NO. 75 (NZ) SQUADRON

"TO SAVE MANKIND - YOURSELF YOU SCORNED TO SAVE"

WARRANT OFFICER CLASS II ROBERT ERNEST TOD DFM
WIRELESS OPERATOR/AIR GUNNER (RCAF), NO. 75 (NZ) SQUADRON

BOTH DIED 23RD JUNE 1943, AGED 23
BURIED MEDEMBLIK GENERAL CEMETERY, NETHERLANDS

Relatively little is known about the Tod brothers, but one thing is certain: they were twins. Raised in Manitoba, they have consecutive service numbers, meaning they enlisted together. It is thought that they may have been identical twins and were clearly inseparable. They trained together and both were assigned to No. 75 (NZ) Squadron on arrival in England.

It is said that they refused to be separated, arguing that one simply could not function without the other. Although strictly against the rules, one can imagine their commanding officer being sympathetic to their pleas. Little did he realise he would have a very difficult letter to write to their mother in the future.

Ernie and Doug's first brush with fate came on 10 April 1943 during an attack on Frankfurt. Their aircraft was damaged by anti-aircraft fire and suffered significant damage whilst still over enemy territory and was later involved in a running battle with German night fighters. During the return flight their aircraft gradually lost height, suggesting that one or more engines may have been damaged. Sensing that it was doubtful they would successfully regain the English coast Ernie (who was the wireless operator) maintained contact with base, giving them accurate indications of their exact whereabouts, allowing plans for their rescue to be made.[138]

Their Stirling bomber eventually ditched three miles off Shoreham by Sea. Owing to Ernie's unswerving devotion to duty, for which he was later awarded an immediate Distinguished Flying Medal[139], the entire crew were picked up by a launch just fifteen minutes later, all unharmed.

Tragically, less than three months later, the Tods' luck ran out. On the night of 22/23 June 1943 their Stirling was one of 557 aircraft detailed for an attack on Mülheim. They had barely reached occupied territory when the aircraft was engaged by night fighters and shot down into the Ijsselmeer Estuary in the Netherlands.

The twins, 23, lie side by side in Medemblik General Cemetery. They are similarly side by side on Panel 254 at the International Bomber Command Centre and, as with all Manitoban losses, they are also commemorated by a natural memorial: Tod Lake, east of Reindeer Lake.[140]

Fittingly for twins, their epitaphs are taken from the last lines of consecutive verses of *O Valiant Hearts* by Sir John Stanhope Arkwright.

J'AI DONNE MA VIE POUR VOUS, DONNEZ-MOI UNE PRIERE. ADIEU, BIEN CHERS PARENTS

WARRANT OFFICER CLASS I JOSEPH CLAUDE ALBERT LABERGE
AIR BOMBER (RCAF), NO. 429 (BISON) SQUADRON
DIED 23RD JUNE 1943, AGED 21
BURIED REICHSWALD FOREST WAR CEMETERY, GERMANY

Translation from French
I GAVE MY LIFE FOR YOU, GIVE ME A PRAYER. GOODBYE, DEAR PARENTS

Joseph was born to Eugene and Helen Laberge, of Dorval, Province of Quebec, Canada, on 28th July 1922. Enlisting on 12th May 1941 Joseph's records show him as a being 'A good physical specimen and fit for aircrew' and 'Understands English well—speaks it fairly well'. His hobby was noted as 'model aeroplane building', indeed part of his education was spent studying aeronautics, but when he started flying training it became clear he was not suited to handling the controls of an aircraft. A report from No. 4 Elementary Flying Training School ending 'Definitely not pilot material'. Joseph underwent air gunnery training although he would ultimately take up bomb aiming duties.[141]

Following a period with French Canadian No. 425 (Alouette) Squadron in 1942, Joseph arrived at No. 429 (Bison) Squadron in June the following year, losing his life, along with the rest of his crew, on the raid to Mülheim on the night of 22/23 June. After the war, five graves in the North Military Cemetery Düsseldorf, identified as being that of a Wellington crew which crashed on 23 June, were exhumed. Initially only the bodies of pilot Joseph Savard, navigator John Macintyre, and air gunner Joseph Bonenfant could be positively identified. The identities of Joseph Laberge and wireless operator/air gunner John Allen were confirmed following further investigation. All were reburied in the Reichswald Forest War Cemetery.

In a letter to the RCAF Chief of the Air Staff on 11 March 1950, Lieutenant Colonel D.E. Macintyre DSO MC, father of John Macintyre, wrote.

> I am well acquainted with the wonderful work of the Commission, having seen many of their cemeteries in France, and I know that the task of beautifying the graves and caring for them will be safe in their hands. Like many others, however, I greatly regret the decision to establish this cemetery in the land of our enemies instead of on friendly soil where the local inhabitants could be counted upon to take an interest as they do in Holland.[142]

Reichswald Forest War Cemetery

The largest Commonwealth cemetery in Germany, containing airmen brought in from numerous burial sites after the Second World War.

TO THE WORLD AN AIRMAN,
TO ME THE WORLD

SERGEANT LESLIE ALFRED TAYLOR
FLIGHT ENGINEER (RAF), NO. 51 SQUADRON
DIED 26TH JULY 1943, AGED 32
BURIED BERGEN GENERAL CEMETERY, NETHERLANDS

The choice of epitaph alludes to the fact that behind the enormous casualty statistics associated with Bomber Command there are individuals. The total loss numbers are a summary, an accumulation. Each and every number, however, represents an individual with character and personality, in relationships with family or partners. To many, who were left to grieve, that person was their world. Leslie was the son of Frederick and Emily Taylor from Cardiff and was married to Katherine. The direct and individual nature of the epitaph suggests it was Katherine's choice of words.

Leslie, as flight engineer on pilot Flying Officer John Cole's 51 Squadron Halifax, took part in the opening raid of what became known as The Battle of Hamburg. Returning from the raid on 24/25 July the crew could report that the 'target area was a mass of flames, and a large pall of smoke was coming up almost to the height of the aircraft.' On return from the raid, and nearing Cuxhaven the Monica tail warning radar alerted the crew and the rear gunner sighted what he believed was a Messerschmitt Bf 109. Enemy searchlights then illuminated the fighter above and astern of the Halifax, and at 500 yards range the rear gunner fired a short burst, maintaining the firing when John Cole threw the bomber into a corkscrew. The Me109 turned away without opening fire. Having landed at 0444 hours on 25 July, within less than eighteen hours they would be airborne again, detailed to attack Essen, the Operations Record Book subsequently recording, 'Nothing further was heard of this machine.'[143]

    Just after midnight Leslie's Halifax was shot down by a night fighter and crashed into the North Sea, near Ijmuiden, with a total loss of life. Between 7 and 13 August the crew washed ashore on the Dutch coast.[144] Leslie and his pilot now rest in Bergen General Cemetery. Three of the crew lie in Castricum Protestant Churchyard, with the remaining two crew members in Bergen-op-Zoom Canadian War Cemetery and Vlieland General Cemetery respectively.

ALSO BABY SON THOMAS FRANCIS BORN AFTER HIS FATHER'S DEATH. DIED AGE SEVEN MONTHS. "UNSEEN THEY'RE NEAR ME"

WARRANT OFFICER THOMAS SIDNEY HEYES DFM
PILOT (RAFVR), NO. 22 OPERATIONAL TRAINING UNIT
DIED 7TH AUGUST 1943, AGED 29
BURIED MANCHESTER (PHILIPS PARK) CEMETERY

The tragedy of this epitaph needs no explanation. Thomas had completed a full tour of operations with No. 429 (Bison) Squadron, a Canadian unit stationed at RAF East Moor, a few miles north of York. He had arrived at the unit on 12 January 1943 and flew his first operation a little over a month later to the French port of Lorient, which was used extensively by the Germans both for shipping and submarines.[145]

A further twenty operations followed between then and the end of June, at which point Thomas was screened from operations, taking up the slightly less risky role of pilot instructor at No. 22 OTU, stationed at RAF Wellesbourne Mountford in Warwickshire. He was recommended for a non-immediate DFM for successfully completing his tour, although it didn't appear in *The London Gazette* until 10 September, a month after his death.[146] (Note that it is often said that DFMs and DFCs were awarded posthumously, which was not possible at the time for these particular decorations. What is invariably meant by this is that they were awarded during the airman's lifetime but not promulgated until after his death.)

By the time Thomas was screened from operations, his wife Elizabeth (née Martin) was expecting their first child. Tragically, Thomas would not survive to see the birth of his son, Thomas Francis.

On 7 August 1943 he was detailed to take Canadian pupil pilot Sergeant W. G. Hill on a night-time 'circuits and bumps' training exercise, together with three other trainees. On their second circuit, the magneto failed in the starboard engine of their Vickers Wellington. Unable to maintain altitude on the one good engine, the pilot was forced to pull up to avoid a high hedge, stalling as a result and crashing in a stubble field about a mile short of the runway.

Thomas' body was returned to his family and he was buried in Manchester (Philips Park) Cemetery, whereas the others were laid to rest close to the station, in Stratford-on-Avon Cemetery.[147] In 1944 Elizabeth, together with her son, attended an investiture at Buckingham Palace to receive the DFM and Thomas Jr. was pictured in the Manchester newspapers wearing it. Less than three months later, Thomas Jr. also died and was laid to rest in his father's grave.

"THEY HAVE NOT DIED, THEY ARE BUT GLORIFIED"

FLYING OFFICER ROBERT THOMAS HOOD DFM
AIR GUNNER (RAAF), NO. 156 SQUADRON
DIED 3RD SEPTEMBER 1943, AGED 23
BURIED CAMBRIDGE CITY CEMETERY, UNITED KINGDOM

Australian Robert Hood was already part way through his training when he married Joyce Watts in May 1941. Ten weeks later Robert set sail for Vancouver, then crossed Canada and the Atlantic, arriving in the United Kingdom at the end of September. Via No. 27 Operational Training Unit, Robert joined No. 460 (RAAF) Squadron in May 1942, ultimately completing twenty-eight operations, and awarded a Distinguished Flying Medal. His citation reads.

> Flight Sergeant Hood has been employed as rear gunner in one of the outstanding crews of the squadron. The successes achieved are due in a large measure to the keenness and alertness of this airman. His excellent directions, coolness and presence of mind have enabled the pilot on many occasions to evade enemy opposition and to complete the mission.[148]

On 9 July 1943 the No. 156 Squadron diary recorded that 'P/O Hood (A/Gnr) reported for flying duties'. At the end of the month, with Canadian pilot Clifford Foderingham DFC, Robert flew his first operations with the squadron, as part of the devastating Battle of Hamburg. Raids to German and Italian targets followed in August, then mid-morning on 3 September the crew, minus a flight engineer, and without any parachutes, took off for an air-to-air firing exercise. A Corporal J.H. Woodman witnessed the fate of the aircraft, which crashed near Kenninghall, Norfolk. 'When I looked up it was at a height I should put at 2,000 ft. or under … It had its nose down very steeply, the impression I got was of a kids toy on a string'. Woodman turned to a colleague saying, "He's leaving it a bit late to pull out". 'Whilst I was saying it I got the impression of slight piveting [sic] turn of the wings, but neither wing was down. We then realised a crash was inevitable … The explosion was like a bomb explosion – a perfect column of flame, smoke and debris straight into the air.'[149] There were no survivors, and all six airmen now rest in Cambridge City Cemetery.

A GREAT INNINGS, PAL

SERGEANT JACK EDWARD FRAZER
AIR GUNNER (RAAF), NO. 16 OPERATIONAL TRAINING UNIT
DIED 28TH SEPTEMBER 1943, AGED 19
BURIED OXFORD (BOTLEY) CEMETERY

There are at least three epitaphs in this book that convey gentle humour, all of which belong to Australian airmen (see also Flight Sergeants John Glen Dening and Louis Michael Gabriel Baker DFM).

Jack was born in April 1924 and raised in Kew, a suburb of Melbourne, Victoria. He enlisted before the age of eighteen and was given a precursory written course until he came of age. In the meantime, he had been working as a farm labourer both on his father's land and neighbouring farms. His father, Clive Eglington Frazer, had first been a lieutenant with the 53rd Battalion during the First World War, later transferring to the Royal Flying Corps, and was still serving in the RAAF with the rank of flying officer when Jack enlisted on 18 July 1942 – just two days after his eighteenth birthday.[150]

On his attestation papers he listed his sporting interests as cricket first – probably accounting for his epitaph – followed by football, tennis, swimming, shooting, riding and athletics.

During initial training Jack was considered for pilot training but was deemed too short, so re-mustered as an air gunner. He embarked for the United Kingdom in July 1943 and was posted to No. 16 OTU RAF Upper Heyford on arrival. Two months later, on 28 September, he and four other trainees were detailed for a Bullseye exercise (a mock bombing attack to prepare new crews for operations). During the exercise they broke cloud at around 800 – 900 feet to establish their position and flew into the ground at Whittlebury, close to the famous Silverstone Circuit, which at the time was itself a newly opened RAF station and home base for No. 17 OTU.

In 2018, the villagers of Whittlebury placed a memorial plaque adjacent to the war memorial on the village green to this and another crew in training that crashed in the parish.[151] It reads:

IN MEMORY OF THE 11 YOUNG AIRMEN WHO LOST THEIR LIVES WHEN
THEIR PLANES LN532 AND LP172 CRASHED IN WHITTLEBURY
ON THE 29TH SEPTEMBER 1943 AND 6TH MAY 1944.

"MAN'S INHUMANITY TO MAN MAKES COUNTLESS THOUSANDS MOURN"

SERGEANT PHILIP MAURICE LAY
PILOT (RAFVR), NO. 15 OPERATIONAL TRAINING UNIT
DIED 2ND OCTOBER 1943, AGED 22
BURIED NORWICH CEMETERY, UNITED KINGDOM

The Second World War had just entered its fifth year when Philip Lay lost his life. Already thousands of Bomber Command airmen had lost their lives, with countless thousands in mourning. In the remaining year-an-a-half of the conflict thousands more would die in the air battle, both those on operations and in training, and thousands more would grieve their passing. On 2 October 1943 Philip's crew were detailed for a cross-country exercise, taking off from RAF Hampstead Norris at 1101 hours. The weather deteriorated and almost an hour-and-a-half later the Wellington crashed into a hill in the north Pennines to the east of Penrith. A framed scroll in Westgate village hall commemorates the crash.

In memory of The crew of Wellington LN497, Who gave their lives on Westernhope Moor On the 2nd October 1943,	Burial location and epitaph
Plt/Officer J.R. Bannan, age 31.	Grimsby (Scartho Road) Cemetery R.I.P.
Sgt T. Churn, age 20.	Beaconsfield Cemetery, Buckinghamshire ETERNAL REST GIVE UNTO HIM, O LORD; AND LET PERPETUAL LIGHT SHINE UPON HIM
Sgt K.T. Creamer, age 22	Harrogate (Stonefall) Cemetery "BUT, CONTENT WITH LITTLE THINGS MADE AN EARTH AND IT WAS WELL"
Sgt P.M. Lay, age 22	Norwich Cemetery, Norfolk "MAN'S INHUMANITY TO MAN MAKES COUNTLESS THOUSANDS MOURN"
Sgt L. Nichol, age 19	Bradford (Scholemoor) Cemetery HIS PRESENCE WE MISS HIS MEMORY WE TREASURE
Sgt D. Postlethwaite, age 34	Rochdale Cemetery (No epitaph)

They gave their tomorrows for our today

The epitaph is from Scottish poet Robert Burns' *Man was Made to Mourn,* a lament on class inequality, which Philip Lay's family have used in a context of loss through war.

HE GAVE HIS ALL, THE GIFT OF HIS UNFINISHED SELF

SERGEANT ARTHUR BAILEY
WIRELESS OPERATOR (RAFVR), NO. 9 (IX) SQUADRON
DIED 8TH OCTOBER 1943, AGED 23
BURIED DURNBACH WAR CEMETERY, GERMANY

Relatives of military casualties often turn to the theme of self-sacrifice when choosing words to commemorate their loss. Arthur, the young son of Francis and Mary Bailey, who volunteered to serve as aircrew, was not yet finished. To his parents he had so much of his life ahead of him. Arthur gave the potential of his future life. It was his gift to all those left behind, and perhaps Arthur's parents found biblical inspiration, drawing upon the sacrifice of Jesus Christ.

Having completed operations to Hagen and Frankfurt earlier in the month, Arthur, his American pilot First Lieutenant Eric Roberts, and their crew were detailed for a raid to Stuttgart on the night of 7/8 October 1943. Having taken off at 2058 hours Lancaster ED836 crashed at Kiechlinsbergen, with only one man surviving.

In May 1947 a report from the Officer Commanding No. 2 Missing Research and Enquiry Unit, following a visit to the cemetery, noted that grave '397', was marked 'Hier ruht der englische Flieger R.J. Darby Erk.M 13244747 8-10/43' (Robert Darby was one of the air gunners on the crew) and grave '346' was marked 'Hier ruht drei unbekannte englische Flieger, 8/10/43.' Not satisfied that there were only 'drei' unknown flyers in the grave, the report noted that 'Exhumation has been requested for grave 346 as it is considered that it may contain the remains of the more than 3 members of the crew.' This appeared to be the case as in August 1948 Arthur Bailey and four of his colleagues were reburied in collective grave 1.D.19-21 at Durnbach War Cemetery and Robert Darby was laid to rest in his own individual grave.

TEARS IN MY EYES EVER GLISTEN;
MY HEART IS ALWAYS SAD FOR THE HUBBY I LOVED – LORNA

SERGEANT EDWIN CARTER
WIRELESS OPERATOR/ AIR GUNNER (RAFVR), NO. 7 SQUADRON
DIED 21ST OCTOBER 1943, AGED 21
BURIED GIETEN GENERAL CEMETERY, NETHERLANDS

Lorna King was born in Brighton on 6 November 1924. The 1939 Register lists her as a shop assistant, yet she was only fourteen years of age. She married Edwin at the age of seventeen. But perhaps the most surprising aspect is that she became a widow at just eighteen. Surprising, but also sobering in equal measure.

Edwin was not much older, having married Lorna when he was barely twenty. Such were the circumstances of war.

A year after marrying, Edwin was flying with No. 7 Squadron, one of the founder squadrons of the elite Pathfinder Force, whose job it was to mark targets with coloured pyrotechnics for the remainder of the bomber stream to aim at. This was Edwin's sixth operation, his first having been on 16 September to attack railway bridges at Modane; the main thoroughfare for troops being transported between France and Italy.[152]

A little over a month later and the squadron was tasked with the first sizeable attack on the distant city of Leipzig. The weather was described in various accounts as 'appalling' leading to scattered bombing. Edwin's aircraft – a Mark III Lancaster JB175 – was shot down by the formidable night fighter pilot Oberleutnant Heinz-Wolfgang Schnaufer of 12./NJG 1, his second 'abschuss' (victory) of the night and one of 121 during the war.[153] (See also Flying Officers Arne Helvard, Earle Garai and Geoffrey Pinn).

Lorna met Reginald Thomas and married him late in 1945.[154] These too were the circumstances of war.

WILL SOME KIND HAND PLACE A FLOWER HERE FOR US. REMEMBERED BY FATHER & MOTHER. R.I.P.

SERGEANT GEORGE PROSSER FINLAY
WIRELESS OPERATOR/AIR GUNNER (RAFVR), NO. 158 SQUADRON
DIED 22ND OCTOBER 1943, AGED 21
BURIED ROTTERDAM (CROOSWIJK) GENERAL CEMETERY, NETHERLANDS

This epitaph reminds us that in the years following the end of the Second World War, overseas travel was out of reach for most people, both financially and practically. It may have been many years after their loved one's deaths that the parents and wives of many airmen were able to visit their graves. Many never did.

It is not known whether Charles and Elizabeth, George's parents, were ever able to make that journey and lay a flower themselves, but it is to be hoped they did.

George and his six comrades had arrived at RAF Lissett, home of No. 158 Squadron, on 8 September 1943, having completed their training with No. 1663 Heavy Conversion Unit.[155] Just a week later they were flying their first 'op' to bomb the Dunlop factory at Montluçon in central France comprising 369 aircraft – a successful attack with mercifully light losses.

Another week later the crew formed part of a much larger attack on Hanover comprising 711 aircraft, which the No. 158 Squadron ORB claims was a great success but in fact was well off target due to stronger than expected winds in the target area.

Exactly one month later – a very long period for this point in the war – came George's next and as it would turn out, final operation, this time to Kassel and with a different captain. The German night fighter controller had successfully anticipated where the bomber stream was headed and fighters awaited their arrival, resulting in heavy losses amounting to some forty-three aircraft (7.6% of the force).[156] Despite this, the attack was devastatingly effective with three V-1 flying bomb factories being destroyed, undoubtedly limiting the scale of the V-1 program.

George's aircraft was shot down by flak and crashed at Goudswaard, south-west of Rotterdam, Netherlands. All were laid to rest in consecutive plots in Rotterdam (Crooswijk) General Cemetery.

DO NOT ASK US IF WE MISS HIM
THERE IS SUCH A VACANT SPACE

FLIGHT SERGEANT BERTRAM GEORGE TUCKER DFM
AIR GUNNER (RAFVR), NO. 83 SQUADRON
DIED 23RD NOVEMBER 1943, AGED 27
BURIED BERLIN 1939-1945 WAR CEMETERY, GERMANY

Bertram Tucker, the son of Frederick and Lilian Tucker, was certainly familiar with raids on the 'Big City', as Berlin was known to the air crews. In the previous couple of months, he had already taken part in four attacks on Berlin flying with his regular captain Pilot Officer D.N. Britton. Bertram was certainly in the thick of the air battle, involved in raids on numerous other targets, and following a raid to Leipzig on 20/21 October the squadron diary would record that his crews, 'little 'do' was shaky indeed.' A fighter, 'made three or four attacks shooting away starboard tail plane, port flaps and a portion of the port main plane. The port outer engine was knocked out, the port tyre flat, the rear turret was u/s after the first attack and the mid-upper turret was damaged.'[157]

At the beginning of November 1943, a new commanding officer arrived at No. 83 Squadron, the diary recording, 'We were very glad to be able to welcome our new C.O. … W/Cdr Hilton needs no introduction to the Squadron his capable handling of tactics whilst at Group has made him well known to all and the fact that he is an ex Flight Commander of the Squadron enables us to welcome a wanderer back to the fold.'

Having returned from a raid to Berlin the night before, flying with his regular pilot, Betram Tucker was then detailed to take up air gunner duties with the highly decorated (DSO, DFC and Bar) and very experienced new CO for a raid on 23/24 November. The squadron diarist noted, 'Berlin again, with no respite for the Hun.' But toward the end of the entry for that day they would also record, 'A severe blow to the squadron was the non-return of our CO Wing Commander Hilton with his crew.' Hit by flak there were no survivors, and the respective graves concentration report form records all seven of the crew originally buried in Doeberitz Standortfriedhof, before being exhumed and relocated to Berlin (Heerstrasse) British War Cemetery, as it was known then, in October 1946.

TOUJOURS PRET POUR DIEU MES PARENTS, MA PATRIE. AVE MARIA

FLIGHT SERGEANT JOSEPH JULES JEAN JACQUES VENNES
AIR BOMBER (RCAF), NO. 23 OPERATIONAL TRAINING UNIT
DIED 25TH NOVEMBER 1943, AGED 21
BURIED PERSHORE CEMETERY, UNITED KINGDOM

Translation from French
ALWAYS READY FOR GOD MY PARENTS, MY HOMELAND. HAIL MARY

On the night of 25/26 November 1943 French Canadian Joseph Vennes was flying with four Canadian colleagues on a night flying practice, taking off from RAF Stratford at 2108 hours. An hour and three quarters later, whilst circling the airfield trying to land, their Wellington crashed with only the rear gunner surviving, whose report into the subsequent enquiry paints a harrowing picture of his crewmates' last moments.

> On the first approach the 'green' was received and when starting to hold off for landing, the aircraft started to shake and vibrate. The engines were then opened up very slowly by the pilot and height was only gained at a very slow rate of climb; finally at 2,000 feet the pilot levelled out. On the downwind leg the second 'green' was obtained but about two seconds afterwards the pilot said 'fire off a red' and then warned the crew to take up their crash positions. This he repeated twice and a short time later said that he was unable to hold the aircraft any longer and started to scream. The aircraft then went into a dive followed by what appeared to be a spin to the starboard. The rear gunner's turret was working the entire time and he swung the turret to port. Just before the dive started the aircraft was vibrating very badly and the engines appeared to be going slowly.[158]

The Report on Flying Accident concluded that the accident, 'was entirely due to failure of one engine'. In letters to the next of kin from the group captain at RAF Pershore he stated that the crash was 'a severe one' and that 'it may be of some consolation for you to know' that their respective husband or son 'must have been killed instantly'. All four Canadians rest in Pershore Cemetery.

(The Commonwealth War Graves Commission website notes the date of death as 26 November 1943, but the flying accident report records that the crash took place prior to midnight on 25 November, with the fatalities 'killed instantly'.)

TELL ENGLAND, YE WHO PASS THIS MONUMENT, WE DIED FOR HER, AND HERE WE REST CONTENT

FLYING OFFICER JAMES PETER JULIAN JENKINS
NAVIGATOR (RAFVR), NO. 106 SQUADRON
DIED 26TH NOVEMBER 1943, AGED 27
BURIED DURNBACH WAR CEMETERY, GERMANY

The Greek poet Simonides is accredited with an epitaph commemorating the heroic last stand by three hundred Spartans killed at the Battle of Thermopylae in 480 BC, 'Go tell the Spartans, thou who passest by, That here, obedient to their laws, we lie.' British journalist and poet Fydell Edmund Garrett took this as inspiration for an epitaph that features on many Second Boer War graves and memorials.

> Tell England, ye who pass this monument,
> We, who died serving her, rest here content.

Novelist Ernest Raymond took this as inspiration for the title of his book *Tell England*, published in 1922, and set pre and during the First World War, which tells the story of how a young schoolboy, Rupert Ray, and his friends meet the news of war with excitement, before encountering reality and death in Gallipoli and France. Near the end of the book Rupert states, 'Oh, but if I go down, I want to ask you not to think it anything but a happy ending. It will be happy, because victory came to the nation, and that is more important than the life of any individual.'[159]

On the night of 22/23 October, James, and his pilot Jacques Hoboken were on a raid to Kassel. The squadron diary records.

> Attacked by fighter and severely damaged – R/G [rear gunner] seriously wounded, five others including pilot also wounded. Fighter driven off but attacked again, inflicting further damage. Fighter eventually evaded, pilot flew crippled aircraft back to Base – unable to land owing to weather. Finally executed masterful landing at Coleby Grange. Excellent performance was given by captain and entire crew.

For their actions that night James' pilot and flight engineer were awarded a DFC and DFM respectively.

With different air gunners, James's crew would fail to return just over a month later, on a raid to Berlin, crashing at Gross-Karben, to the south of the 'Big City'. Originally buried in Gross-Karben civilian cemetery the entire crew would be reburied in Durnbach War Cemetery in September 1947.

"WITH THE WINGS OF A BIRD AND THE HEART OF A MAN HE COMPASS'D HIS FLIGHT"

FLIGHT LIEUTENANT FRANCIS GEORGE TIMS COLLINS
NAVIGATOR (RAFVR), NO. 101 SQUADRON
DIED 27TH NOVEMBER 1943, AGED 28
BURIED DURNBACH WAR CEMETERY, GERMANY

The Greek myth of Icarus, who tragically fell to his death having flown too close to the sun, proved an inspiration for poets across the ages. The myth suggests that Icarus, despite warnings, became a victim of excessive ambition. Francis Tims Collins' family chose a quote from the pre-war poem *The New Icarus* by the prolific writer and editor Ernest Rhys, which asks the reader to take a more heroic view of the 'new' aviators.

> With the wings of a bird and the heart of a man he compass'd his flight,
> And the cities and seas, as he flew, were like smoke at his feet.
> He lived a great life while we slept, in the dark of the night,
> And went home by the mariners' road, down the stars' empty street.

Francis Tims Collins was clearly a highly educated man. His name is recorded on the Second World Memorial in the Chapel Passage at Balliol Chapel, University of Oxford, and as a prolific chess player he made a name for himself pre-war, winning numerous titles. The March 1944 edition of *CHESS* magazine, under the title 'Tims Collins Missing' reported, 'According to Mr Du Mont, FG Tims Collins is reported missing from a bombing raid. How we hope that this genial and universally popular chess congress-ite managed to bale out!'[160]

Francis was the navigator on a No. 101 Squadron Lancaster that was lost on the Berlin raid of 26/27 November 1943. From the crew of eight only two men would survive. Originally buried in Frankfurt Main Cemetery all six were moved to Durnbach War Cemetery with only one casualty given his own grave and Francis Tims Collins and four others placed in a collective grave. The two survivors from the loss became prisoners but tragically the special equipment officer, Canadian George Spofford, who had operated the radio jamming Airborne Cigar (ABC) equipment, took his own life in captivity the following year.

"NOW I AM DEAD, BUT LIVE, LIVE IN YOUR LIFE AND LOVE"
J.F.B.

SERGEANT JOHN FRANCIS BURTON
PILOT (RAFVR), NO. 16 OPERATIONAL TRAINING UNIT
DIED 27TH NOVEMBER 1943, AGED 20
BURIED OXFORD (BOTLEY) CEMETERY, UNITED KINGDOM

An inscription almost certainly based on the final words of John Burton's last letter, judging by the signature. All airmen were required to write such a letter before they began flying operations in the face of the enemy, in case the worst should happen, and those epitaphs which may be identified as such usually offer hope about the future to their loved ones.

Born to English parents William and Dorothy Burton, originally of Urmston, Manchester, the family had been living in Argentina, where William was a senior accountant at Southern, Western and Midlands Railways.

John was first educated at The Saint Andrew's Scots School (Escuela Escocesa San Andrés) in Olivos, Buenos Aires until December 1931. He then continued his education in the UK in early 1932, initially joining Godwin College in Cliftonville (near Margate) where he stayed until July 1933 followed by Sutton Valence School, Maidstone as a boarder, where he gained a Higher Certificate. He represented the school in several sports throughout his time at Sutton Valence, rising to be captain of the first XI football team. He was also a member of the dramatic society and was awarded prizes for Latin and History before leaving to attend Peterhouse College, Cambridge University as an RAF Cadet.[161]

He took off from RAF Upper Heyford, Oxfordshire at 0421 hours on 27 November 1943 for a high-level bombing practice over the Preston Capes ranges. Twelve minutes after take-off the aircraft dived and crashed near Culworth, 16 miles south-west of Northampton, exploding on impact.[162] The five-man crew all perished. Some were buried locally whereas others were returned to their hometowns.[163]

John's name may also be found on the Roll of Honour at the English Social Club, Lomas de Zamora, Argentina, in the central stained glass window of the chapel in the Llavallol Cemetery, at St. John the Baptist Anglican Cathedral in Buenos Aires and at St. Andrew's Presbyterian Church, also in Buenos Aires.[164]

(He is one of two airmen with Argentinian connections featured in this work. See also Sergeant William Thomas McDonald.)

". . . AND LEFT THE VIVID AIR SIGNED WITH THEIR HONOUR"

SERGEANT STANLEY LIONEL INGLE
WIRELESS OPERATOR/AIR GUNNER (RAFVR), NO. 103 SQUADRON
DIED 27TH NOVEMBER 1943, AGED 20
BURIED HARROGATE (STONEFALL) CEMETERY, UNITED KINGDOM

In seeking to remember Stanley Ingle's loss as having occurred whilst undertaking a heroic pursuit, the family drew upon Stephen Spender's poem *The Truly Great* which opens with the line, 'I think continually of those who were truly great'. Spender goes on to consider the heroes of the past, and what made them heroic. They would 'Never to allow gradually the traffic to smother with noise and fog, the flowering of the spirit'. They were individuals, 'who in their lives fought for life, who wore at their hearts the fire's centre'. And ultimately, 'Born of the sun, they travelled a short while toward the sun and left the vivid air signed with their honour.'[165]

At a ceremony commemorating the fortieth anniversary of the D-Day landings on 6 June 1984, and attended by many veterans, President of the United States Ronald Reagan quoted the same poem:

> Gentlemen, I look at you and I think of the words of Stephen Spender's poem. You are men who in your lives fought for life... and left the vivid air signed with your honour.

Stanley Ingle's aircraft was one of 443 Lancasters that were sent to Berlin on the night of 26/27 November 1943. A fierce air battle developed and 28 Lancasters were lost. For those that returned to more friendly skies hazards remained. Many had been damaged by enemy action, with the danger compounded by poor weather conditions. On the same night a smaller bombing force had been sent to Stuttgart, finding similar difficult conditions on their return.

Having taken off just after half-past five on the evening of 26 November, from RAF Elsham Wolds, Stanley's crew met poor weather on their return in the early hours the following day. It is believed they had been diverted to RAF Middleton St. George, subsequently trying to land at the same time as a No. 428 Squadron Halifax. A flying accident report noted, 'Neither aircraft obeyed the A.C.P's red Aldis warnings', and that at 0110 hours, 'Collision took place at approximately 200 feet to the windward of the funnel.' Only one of Stanley's colleagues survived, injured, with a total loss of life in the 428 Squadron crew.

HE GAVE THE WHITE FLOWER OF A BLAMELESS LIFE

FLIGHT SERGEANT JOHN IRVINE MCKEE
WIRELESS OPERATOR (RAAF), NO. 460 (AUSTRALIAN) SQUADRON
DIED 2ND DECEMBER 1943, AGED 23
BURIED BERLIN 1939-1945 WAR CEMETERY, GERMANY

Alfred, Lord Tennyson's poem *Idylls of the King* published over a time span of twenty-six years, tells the story of King Arthur and the members of his court. Written in the Victorian age it draws upon the period ideals of what it meant to be a chivalrous and noble gentleman. During the writing, and a year after the passing of Prince Albert, Consort to Queen Victoria, Tennyson dedicated the poem to the much-loved and admired prince, the 'ideal knight … whose glory was, redressing human wrong'.

The McKee family turned to the 'Dedication' for their son's epitaph. There was much to draw on, their final choice being a slight adaption of the final line from this excerpt.

> We have lost him: he is gone:
> We know him now: all narrow jealousies
> Are silent; and we see him as he moved,
> How modest, kindly, all-accomplished, wise,
> With what sublime repression of himself,
> And in what limits, and how tenderly;
> Not swaying to this faction or to that;
> Not making his high place the lawless perch
> Of winged ambitions, nor a vantage-ground
> For pleasure; but through all this tract of years
> Wearing the white flower of a blameless life …

It would appear, from the No. 460 (RAAF) Squadron diary, that John's crew arrived at RAF Binbrook at the end of November 1943, and this was their first operational flight.[166] The squadron would lose five Lancasters on the Berlin raid of 2/3 December, and in addition to the deaths of twenty-seven aircrews, two reporters were also killed, Norwegian war correspondent Nordhal Greig and Norman Stockton reporting for *The Sydney Sun*. The graves concentration report form records that John was initially buried in Marlow Cemetery, Germany, with the rest of his crew, from which they were all exhumed and reburied in the 'Berlin (Heerstasse) British War Cemetery' (Berlin 1939-1945 War Cemetery) on 23 November 1946.

"I PRAY THAT ALL WHO SURVIVE WILL MAKE SURE THAT WE DID NOT DIE IN VAIN AND THAT THEY WILL BANISH ALL CAUSES OF WAR FOREVER"

SERGEANT FREDERICK NICHOLS
WIRELESS OPERATOR (RAFVR), NO. 16 OPERATIONAL TRAINING UNIT
DIED 11TH DECEMBER 1943, AGED 21
BURIED OXFORD (BOTLEY) CEMETERY, UNITED KINGDOM

Frederick Nichols' crew for their night cross-country of 11 December consisted of a fellow British national, three Canadians, a Norwegian airman, and an Australian pilot. Approximately five and a half hours into their flight, from RAF Upper Heyford, their Wellington was being plotted by members of the Royal Observer Corps, as it circled their post near the village of Little Rollright, Oxfordshire. The crew had also been requesting barometric pressures and the height of the cloud base. Just after 11 pm, heading towards the observer post, the motors were heard to rev up. Within seconds the Wellington smashed into the ground and there was a total loss of life. The investigation into the accident would later note that none of the crew were wearing parachute harnesses, and that 'at the last minute [the pilot] must have seen the trees ahead, opened his throttles, fined the pitch and attempted to turn away from them. This he was unable to do.'[167]

The number of characters in the epitaph far exceeds the sixty requested by the Imperial War Graves Commission, but this is clearly a case of not wishing to cause further distress. Frederick was the son of Bert and Netties Nichols, from Glasgow, and one would assume they submitted the quoted words for the epitaph. Their son played his part in the defeat of Nazism, so in that respect he did not die in vain. Alas, those who survived were not able to prevent further wars.

Frederick rests with his Australian pilot and Canadian colleagues in Oxford (Botley) Cemetery. The second pilot, from Diss, Norfolk, rests in his home town and the body of Norwegian navigator Viktor Møinichen Plahte was eventually returned to his home country, buried in Haslum cemetery, Bærum.

GOD LOVED HIM TOO AND TOOK HIM HOME WITH HIM TO REST. AUF WIEDERSEHEN, LIEBLING

SERGEANT RAYMOND JOHN BARONI
AIR GUNNER (RCAF), NO. 9 (IX) SQUADRON
DIED 16TH DECEMBER 1943, AGED 21
BURIED BERLIN 1939-1945 WAR CEMETERY, GERMANY

Raymond's parents Michael and Marie were the proprietors of *Hotel Hamilton*, Neepawa, Canada. Born in Switzerland Michael and Marie had become naturalised Canadians, and Raymond was born in Winnipeg on 6 December 1922.[168]

In 1947 a Flight Lieutenant MacIntyre of No. 4 MREU, visited Finow cemetery to investigate the loss of Raymond's Lancaster and a 619 Squadron crew who failed to return the same night. MacIntyre, accompanied by two colleagues and a 'Russian Conducting Officer' were shown the graves of the two crews by villagers but, 'owing to the ignorance shown, no one was able to say which bodies had been recovered from which aircraft.' On a communal mound were fourteen crosses numbered twelve to twenty-five. 'Baroni' appeared on cross number 20, and others displayed names, with the rest reading 'Unbekannt' (unknown). It became clear that the bodies had not all been buried individually. Under some crosses there were no bodies. Exhumation enabled MacIntyre to identify Raymond by his identity disc. Four others could also be named, and three could possibly be identified with further investigation. The rest would remain unidentified. John was reburied in the Berlin (Heerstrasse) British Cemetery, as it was known then, in September 1947.

On 21 February 1949, Raymond's mother Marie wrote to the 'Department of National Defence for Air'.

> My dear husband, broken hearted over his youngest son's death, passed away July 1945. His most passionate wish for both of us to visit our sons grave in the near future, was hopeless. I, his widow, have made reservation for Switzerland on the *Empress of Canada* … I would appreciate it if you kindly will advise me if it is at all possible to visit my son's grave in Berlin.

On 1 March Marie received a reply.

> Nothing is known here concerning travel from Switzerland to Berlin, but as you are doubtless aware, all travel from this end to Berlin is by air, and civilian travel is prohibited … as the situation now exists it is highly improbably that you will be able to proceed to Berlin.

At the time of writing the Soviet Union had blockaded all the land routes into the areas of Berlin controlled by the western Allies.

PASS NOT THIS STONE IN SORROW BUT IN PRIDE AND STRIVE TO LIVE AS NOBLY AS HE DIED

WING COMMANDER DAVID WILLIAM HOLFORD DSO DFC
PILOT (RAF), NO. 100 SQUADRON
DIED 16TH-17TH DECEMBER 1943, AGED 22
BURIED CAMBRIDGE CITY CEMETERY, UNITED KINGDOM

On the night of 16/17 December 1943 numerous aircraft found thick fog over the East of England on return from a raid to Berlin. Many aircraft were damaged, manned by tired crews, and most were running short of fuel as they tried to find somewhere to land. Four were abandoned and twenty-six aircraft crashed, including David Holford's Lancaster.

David was just 22-years-old when he died yet was one of the Royal Air Force's most experienced and well regarded bomber pilots. Having joined the RAF pre-war he went on to fly Wellingtons operationally, including taking part in the attack on the *Scharnhorst* and *Gneisenau* on 12 February 1942, for which he awarded the Distinguished Service Order to add to a previously earned Distinguished Flying Cross. In February 1943 David, now married to WAAF Intelligence Officer Jean, was promoted to Wing Commander, one of the youngest airmen in the RAF to ever hold this rank. In November 1943 he was given command of No. 100 Squadron.

On the fateful night of 16/17 December, David's Lancaster was attacked by German night fighters on the way to and from the target. Nearing Waltham (RAF Grimsby), and despite the damage to his Lancaster, David decided to let less experienced crews try and land first. When fuel became critically low he was finally forced to attempt a landing, and hit rising ground near Kelstern. The wireless operator Eric MacKay, having been thrown clear, found his pilot lying in the snow, Holford asking 'The crew ... are the crew all right?'. By the time the ambulance arrived David had passed away.[169]

The station commander at Waltham described David Holford as an 'outstanding personality and squadron commander' and a local GP Dr Thomas Kirk would write, 'David Holford is dead. In one of the crashes that black Thursday night. I feel absolutely wretched. David was the finest of all the young RAF boys - in fact I liked and respected him more than I can say. He had just bought a house near Grimsby for his wife and baby. Is this the way to win the war - by sacrificing all our best? And is all this bombing really shortening the war?'[170]

THERE IS NO DEATH! THE STARS GO DOWN TO RISE UPON SOME FAIRER SHORE

SERGEANT PETER GEORGE HANCOCK
AIR BOMBER (RAFVR), NO. 103 SQUADRON
DIED 20TH DECEMBER 1943, AGED 22
BURIED DURNBACH WAR CEMETERY, GERMANY

Peter and three of his crewmates lost their lives on the raid to Frankfurt on the night of 20/21 December 1943. Having taken off from RAF Elsham Wolds at 1651 hours, their No. 103 Squadron Lancaster fell to a night fighter. The enemy aircraft, damaged by return fire from Sergeant Roberts in the rear turret, would later be shot down by friendly flak.[171] Peter was buried in his own grave at Floersbach Civil Cemetery and his three deceased colleagues in a collective grave in Marjoss Civil Cemetery. All four were transferred to Durnbach War Cemetery in September 1947. The bomb aimer on the crew, Geoffrey Turnbull, managed to escape the stricken Lancaster, but would not survive captivity, tragically losing his life when Allied fighters strafed a POW column a month before the end of the war.[172]

Peter Hancock's family turned to John Luckey McCreery's poem *There Is No Death* for words to express both their loss and hope of life after death. The poem opens with the lines.

> There is no death! the stars go down
> To rise upon some other shore,

Peter's family, perhaps in changing the word 'other', in the second line, to 'fairer' wish to express further optimism. Their son is not just in a different place, but in a better place.

McCreery uses natural imagery throughout the poem as metaphors for an afterlife, such as

> The leaves may fall,
> The flowers may fade and pass away –
> They only wait, through wintry hours,
> The coming of the May.

The poem is hopeful, offering comfort. Those who passed but 'are worthy of our love or care' remain in our memory and in our hearts. The last stanza reads.

> And ever near us, though unseen,
> The dear immortal spirits tread;
> For all the boundless universe
> Is life — there are no dead.

"YET LEAVING HERE A NAME, I TRUST, THAT WILL NOT PERISH IN THE DUST"

SERGEANT THOMAS COOK HENDERSON
AIR GUNNER (RAF), NO. 103 SQUADRON
DIED 29TH DECEMBER 1943, AGED 19
BURIED REICHSWALD FOREST WAR CEMETERY, GERMANY

Thomas' family have chosen the last lines of the poem *My Days among the Dead are Past* by English Romantic poet Robert Southey, which is quoted in full.

My days among the Dead are past;
Around me I behold,
Where'er these casual eyes are cast,
The mighty minds of old;
My never-failing friends are they,
With whom I converse day by day.

With them I take delight in weal,
And seek relief in woe;
And while I understand and feel
How much to them I owe,
My cheeks have often been bedew'd
With tears of thoughtful gratitude.

My thoughts are with the Dead, with them
I live in long-past years,
Their virtues love, their faults condemn,
Partake their hopes and fears,
And from their lessons seek and find
Instruction with an humble mind.

My hopes are with the Dead, anon
My place with them will be,
And I with them shall travel on
Through all Futurity;
Yet leaving here a name, I trust,
That will not perish in the dust.

The poem expresses a connection with those who have passed before, gratitude for their legacy, 'how much to them I owe', and a wish to learn, 'from their lessons', to, 'seek and find instruction with an humble mind'. Thomas Henderson left his name, and the Commonwealth War Graves Commission and International Bomber Command Centre have ensured it will not perish in the dust.

GREATER LOVE HATH NO MAN THAN THIS, THAT A MAN LAY DOWN HIS LIFE FOR HIS FRIENDS

AIRCRAFTMAN 1ST CLASS SIDNEY HERBERT RANCE
GROUNDCREW (RAFVR), NO. 12 OPERATIONAL TRAINING UNIT
DIED 7TH JANUARY 1944, AGED 41
BURIED SANDHURST (ST. MICHAEL) CHURCHYARD, UNITED KINGDOM

Early on the afternoon of 6 January 1944 a Douglas Boston of No. 107 Squadron, returning from an aborted attack on a flying bomb site in France, prepared to land with bombs still on board, but as the squadron diary recorded, 'while on the circuit aircraft L piloted by Lt. Truxler crashed near Little Sandhurst.' There were no survivors from the crew of four, 'We shall miss this experienced crew. They were very pleasant colleagues.'

Eyewitnesses in Little Sandhurst recalled hearing the aircraft in trouble, seeing a plane nosedive down, hearing the crash and seeing smoke and flames. Many rushed to the scene, between the kitchen garden of Eagle House School and 'Ivy Bank' bungalow in Longdown Road, including Sidney Rance who was on leave and lived with his wife Sarah and newborn baby in Little Sandhurst.[173] Vainly attempting to help the crew, and fighting the fires, several of the local people were seriously wounded when the aircraft exploded, including Sidney who, despite receiving hospital treatment, succumbed to his injuries. Sidney's bravery that day was recognised with a Mention in Despatches, the notification appearing in *The London Gazette* on 8 June 1944.

Sidney was buried in his local churchyard. Next to the bottom of his Commonwealth War Graves Commission headstone is another memorial stone reading, REUNITED WITH HIS DEVOTED WIFE SARAH DOROTHY 1908-2001 BOTH SADLY MISSED.

Sidney's epitaph could not be more apt in this circumstance, having taken an extraordinary risk, which ultimately proved fatal, in trying to save his air force colleagues. The words, taken from the Bible and the Gospel of John, Chapter 15, verse 13, often feature as the epitaph on military graves. Indeed, a search of the epitaphs of Bomber Command database reveals 1,266 inscriptions featuring these words, or with slight adaptations.

A CANADIAN IN WHOSE VEINS
FLOWED THE BLOOD OF VIKINGS

FLYING OFFICER FREDERICK JACOB HJARTARSON
NAVIGATOR (RCAF), NO. 1656 HEAVY CONVERSION UNIT
DIED 14TH JANUARY 1944, AGED 22
BURIED BATH (HAYCOMBE) CEMETERY, UNITED KINGDOM

A Canadian citizen Frederick Hjartarson's record of service records his 'racial origin' as being 'Icelandic', his father, Ivar, and mother, Rosa, both born and marrying in Iceland. On 20 January 1944 the commanding officer at RAF Lindholme wrote to Frederick's mother.[174]

> Dear Mrs Hjartarson
> Before you receive this letter, you will have been informed by the Air Ministry of the very sad loss of your son Flying Officer Frederick Hjartarson.
>
> Unfortunately, owing to the time taken to communicate under present conditions, it was not possible to ascertain your wishes regarding the funeral, and I had therefore to arrange for his burial without reference to you. You will, I am sure, understand the necessity of this action, and I sincerely trust that the arrangements we were able to make were what you would have wished.
>
> Your son's funeral is to take place at Bath tomorrow, the 21st January, at 3.30p.m. and his body will be interred in the RAF Cemetery where arrangements have been made for full service honours to be accorded, the coffin being carried by NCOs and covered with the Union Jack. A firing party will be provided, and the Last Post sounded at the end.
>
> Wreaths will be sent from myself and the Officers, NCOs and airmen of this Station. I hope to send you shortly a photograph of the grave.
>
> You will wish to know that all War graves are taken care of by the Imperial War Grave Commission, who will erect a temporary wooden cross, pending the provision of a permanent memorial.
>
> I am instructed to explain also that question of re-interment, if this was desired, could only be considered at the conclusion of hostilities.
>
> May I now express the very deep sympathy which all of us feel with you in the sad loss you have sustained. It may be of some slight comfort to you to know that your son's death was instantaneous and that he died whilst flying in the service of his country.

On 13 January 1944, Frederick and his crew, had been detailed for a five-hour night cross country exercise. Everything appeared to be going well until just after 0100 hours on 14 January. Eyewitnesses would later report that the Handley Page Halifax's engines were behaving irregularly. The pilot gave the order to abandon aircraft, but the Halifax went into a spin, losing height rapidly, crashing near Davidstow Moor, Devon with a total loss of life, all members of the crew found with parachute packs attached to their harnesses.

HE STAYED WITH HIS SHIP, SAVED HIS CREW, AND A VILLAGE. WE ARE JUSTLY PROUD

FLYING OFFICER MARTIN STEWART LITTLE
PILOT (RCAF), NO. 1659 HEAVY CONVERSION UNIT
DIED 25TH MARCH 1944, AGED 23
BURIED BROOKWOOD MILITARY CEMETERY, UNITED KINGDOM

Detailed for a Bullseye (navigational) exercise Martin Little's Halifax strayed over London while an enemy raid was taking place. Problems with the I.F.F. (Identification Friend or Foe) resulted in the bomber being attacked by ground fire. With the aircraft hit and engines put out of operation, Martin fought to keep control and ordered his crew to bail out. On 5 April 1944 air gunner Nick Cowan wrote to Martin's parents.

> To 'Lou', as we knew him, the crew and myself owe our lives to-day. If it had not been for his presence of mind and ability to control an aircraft that was in reality unflyable we would not be here now. Like a true captain he saw that his crew had bailed out in time and because of his unselfishness and determination stayed at the controls and guided his ship over a populated area. In doing so he was too low to jump and as a result he gave up his life. It must seem so unfair and unjust to you, but believe me, you can be justly proud of your son. Disregarding his own safety for that of others he did not die in vain.

On 9 April Kathleen Bethell, who witnessed the crash of Martin's aircraft, wrote from her home in Chorley Wood, Hertfordshire, to the young Canadian's mother.

> For some time I have been meaning to write to you. I so much want you to know how grateful we were to Flying Officer Little's great courage and supreme sacrifice. He will always remain in my memory, because had he not controlled his plane so skilfully and for so long, many of us would have lost our lives. I thanked God when with one supreme effort the plane turned off to the woods and fields beyond and at that moment it burst fully into flame. I do want you to know that help was as soon at the spot as possible and if it was humanly possible Mr Little would have been saved, but he was gone when the policeman arrived, and in his (the policeman's opinion) death was instantaneous. Mr Little was not burned. He was untouched. He fell some distance from his plane. I feel you would like to know this, because I should if it was my husband, or baby daughter.[175]

FLYING OFFICER
M. S. LITTLE
PILOT
ROYAL CANADIAN AIR FORCE
25TH MARCH 1944 AGE 23

E'EN AS HE TROD THAT DAY TO GOD
SO WALKED HE FROM HIS BIRTH...KIPLING

FLIGHT LIEUTENANT THOMAS BARKER LEIGH
AIR GUNNER (RAF), NO. 76 SQUADRON
DIED 31ST MARCH 1944, AGED 25
BURIED POZNAN OLD GARRISON CEMETERY, POLAND

Thomas was one of the prisoners-of-war who took part in the 'Great Escape', the break out from Stalag Luft III, on the night of 24/25 March 1944. Having joined the Royal Air Force in 1935, Thomas trained at RAF Halton (a 'Halton Brat'), and then took up the opportunity to become aircrew early in the war. In 1941, as an air gunner, he joined No. 76 Squadron and on the night of 5/6 August, in the rear turret of a Handley Page Halifax, was shot down over enemy territory. Thomas was captured early the following morning, eventually arriving at Stalag Luft I, Barth before a transfer to Stalag Luft III, Sagan.

Having exited tunnel 'Harry' on the night of the Great Escape, Thomas, enduring the cold and harsh conditions, attempted to distance himself from the prison camp but before the end of the month he was recaptured and taken to Görlitz prison. Of the seventy-six who had escaped from their confines at Stalag Luft III, seventy-three were recaptured, from which fifty were subsequently murdered by the Gestapo. Thomas was one of those shot and his ashes were returned to Sagan in a cremation urn. After the war his remains were reinterred in Poznan Old Garrison Cemetery, alongside those of forty-seven other executed great escapers.

In 1892 writer Rudyard Kipling married American Caroline Balestier. Journalist Wolcott Balestier had collaborated on the book *The Naulahka* with Kipling, and Caroline had come to London to keep house for her brother. In December 1891 Wolcott had fallen victim to typhoid fever, dying in Dresden. Thomas Leigh's epitaph draws upon Kipling's poem *To Wolcott Balestier*, which includes the lines

> E'en as he trod that day to God so walked he from his birth,
> In simpleness and gentleness and honour and clean mirth.

HOW OFT HEREAFTER SHALL WE LOOK THRU THIS SAME WORLD, AFTER YOU - IN VAIN

SERGEANT BERNARD GORDON EASTERLOW
AIR GUNNER (RAFVR), NO. 9 (IX) SQUADRON
DIED 12TH MAY 1944, AGED 21
BURIED WILSELE CHURCHYARD, BELGIUM

The words chosen are a slight adaptation of lines from *The Rubaiyat of Omar Khayyam*, a translation by 19th century poet Edward FitzGerald of verse attributed to the 'Astronomer-Poet of Persia' Omar Khayyam. Long and complex, the poem touches on nature and God, the joys of life and love, but also mortality and death. The poem underwent various revisions, the lines relating to Bernard's epitaph adapted from the ending of this excerpt.

> Alas, that Spring should vanish with the Rose!
> That Youth's sweet-scented Manuscript should close!
> The Nightingale that in the Branches sang,
> Ah, whence, and whither flown again, who knows!

> Ah, Love! could thou and I with Fate conspire
> To grasp this sorry Scheme of Things entire,
> Would not we shatter it to bits—and then
> Re-mould it nearer to the Heart's Desire!

> Ah, Moon of my Delight who know'st no wane,
> The Moon of Heav'n is rising once again:
> How oft hereafter rising shall she look
> Through this same Garden after me—in vain![176]

Bernard's family in changing 'she' to 'we' and 'me' to 'you' personalise the quote, often finding themselves looking back to shared times with someone they loved. But those times are gone. They look back 'in vain'. Bernard was, and always will be, lost.

"OUT OF THIS NETTLE, DANGER, WE PLUCK THIS FLOWER, SAFETY"

FLYING OFFICER GEOFFREY PHILIP PINN
NAVIGATOR (RAAF), NO. 466 (AUSTRALIAN) SQUADRON
DIED 13TH MAY 1944, AGED 22
BURIED SCHOONSELHOF CEMETERY, BELGIUM

An excerpt from a letter penned by a nobleman who refuses to join the rebellion against King Henry and read aloud by Hotspur in William Shakespeare's *Henry IV*, the meaning of which is that it is sometimes necessary to deliberately put oneself in danger in order to obtain something that is to be treasured – safety, or more specifically in this context, peace.

A somewhat different interpretation might be an ironic one, since Neville Chamberlain quoted it on leaving for Munich and his third meeting with Adolph Hitler on 29 September 1938. On his return he triumphantly declared 'Peace for our time' and perhaps this quote rang rather hollow with Geoffrey's loved ones after his death.

Geoffrey Pinn was born on 6 July 1921 and before enlisting was working as a high school teacher in the northern Sydney suburb of Epping. He had gained a Bachelor of Economics degree from the University of Sydney and afterwards studied for a Diploma in Education at the same institute.[177]

He had arrived at No. 466 Squadron, then based at RAF Leconfield in the East Riding of Yorkshire, in April 1944. He flew his first operation on the night of 9/10 May to attack a coastal gun battery at Morsalines on the Cherbourg peninsula, close to what would become Utah beach, less than a month later during the D-Day landings.

Two days later the target was gun positions at Colline-Beaumont, likely as a spoof attack ahead of D-Day, since this is where the Allies wanted Germany to believe the landings would take place. As it turned out, the target proved difficult for the Pathfinder Mosquitoes to mark, resulting in scattered bombing. That was perhaps of little consequence, the very fact that it had been attacked would have been enough to sow the seeds of confusion.

Geoffrey's third operation was the very next night – to attack railway yards at Hasselt in Belgium as part of the Transportation Plan, to hamper the German ability to move reinforcement troops to the Normandy area after D-Day. They were shot down by a night fighter flown by Oberleutnant Heinz-Wolfgang Schnaufer near Turnhout, Belgium, very close to the border with Holland.[178] This is the fourth Schnaufer victory detailed in this book.

Geoffrey's bombing career lasted just four days. His sacrifice, however, is remembered to this day.

LOST TO US FOR 53 YEARS LEFT PAIN AND MANY TEARS
RISEN FROM A BOGGY DEEP COMFORTS US AS YOU SLEEP

PILOT OFFICER FRED ROACH
AIR GUNNER (RCAF), NO. 426 (THUNDERBIRD) SQUADRON
DIED 13TH MAY 1944, AGED 25
BURIED GERAARDSBERGEN COMMUNAL CEMETERY, BELGIUM

One of the most intriguing aspects of The Bomber Command Memorial, in The Green Park, London, is the ceiling, designed to reflect the geodetic structure of the inside of a Wellington bomber, and made of aluminium. The source of some of this aluminium is Fred Roach's No. 426 Squadron Halifax bomber that was shot down in May 1944, near Schendelbeke, Belgium. Fifty-three years later the remains of the aircraft were extricated from a swamp, and a considerable amount of the wreckage returned to Canada. Some of the aluminium, turned into ingots by the Bomber Command Museum of Canada, Nanton, was sent to the United Kingdom on board a No. 429 Squadron C-17 transport to be used in the roof construction of the London memorial. The International Bomber Command Centre, Lincoln, have also incorporated some of the aluminium in their welcome panel.

Halifax LW682 fell to a night fighter on the raid to Leuven on the night of 12/13 May 1944, crashing into a marsh and killing the entire crew of eight. The bodies of five of the airmen were recovered and buried locally. In 1949 Fred Roach's father received a letter from the RCAF Casualties Officer.[179]

> ... I am sorry indeed to have to inform you that no trace can be found of the grave of your son or two members of his crew, Pilot Officer J.W. Summerhayes and Pilot Officer W.B. Bentz both R.C.A.F. and it must be accepted that your son and two members of his crew crashed with their aircraft which you are aware crashed into extremely swampy of boggy ground, disappeared entirely from sight and could not be salvaged and the names of your son, Pilot Officers Summerhayes and Bentz have regretfully registered as not having a "known' grave.

A half a century after the crash Jay Hammond, the nephew of Wilbur Bentz, visited the site of the crash, and initiated the recovery of his uncle's Halifax. Karl Kjarsgaard of Canada's Halifax 57 Rescue, with the assistance of No. 426 Squadron Association and the Belgian Aviation History Association set about reclaiming the wreckage and the missing airmen from the marsh.[180] With the remains of Fred Roach, Wilbur Bentz, and John Summerhayes found, they were finally laid to rest in a collective grave in the communal cemetery at Geraardsbergen, alongside the bodies of their former crewmates.

445195 LEADING A.C.W.
DOROTHY FRANCES JOAN
BAILEY
WOMEN'S AUXILIARY AIR FORCE
13TH MAY 1944 AGE 21

HER BROTHER SYDNEY, SGT.R.A.F. WAS LOST OVER GERMANY 26TH MAY 1943 AGE 21 "WE WILL REMEMBER THEM"

LEADING AIRCRAFTWOMAN DOROTHY FRANCES JOAN BAILEY
WOMEN'S AUXILIARY AIR FORCE
NO. 692 (FELLOWSHIP OF THE BELLOWS) SQUADRON
DIED 13TH MAY 1944, AGED 21
BURIED PLAXTOL CHURCHYARD, UNITED KINGDOM

Dorothy's parents were still dealing with the grief following the loss of their son Sydney, when news came through of the tragic accident that befell their daughter. Dorothy was serving with No. 692 Squadron of No. 8 Group's Light Night Striking Force at the time, based at RAF Graveley, Huntingdonshire. While cycling back to base Dorothy was struck by a motor vehicle and died of her injuries in the 49th American Station Hospital, Diddington Cambridgeshire. Her body was returned to her parents Albert and Frances Bailey and buried in their village churchyard.

The previous year twenty-one-year-old Sydney Bailey's Lancaster failed to return from a raid to Düsseldorf, with a total loss of life in the crew of seven. Syndey and his colleagues were originally buried in Düsseldorf Nordfriedhof prior to reburial in Reichswald Forest War Cemetery. Sydney's parents adapted lines from Laurence Binyon's poem *For the Fallen* for their son's epitaph.

AT THE DAWN AND AT THE SETTING OF THE SUN WE WILL REMEMBER HIM

SERGEANT SYDNEY ARTHUR JAMES BAILEY
AIR GUNNER (RAFVR), NO. 12 SQUADRON
DIED 26TH MAY 1943, AGED 21
BURIED REICHSWALD FOREST WAR CEMETERY, GERMANY

BORN IN HALIFAX, NOVA SCOTIA. OUR DEAR SONS ARE REUNITED. IAN, R.C.A.F. KILLED JANUARY 1943 AND BURIED IN HIS HOME TOWN

WARRANT OFFICER CLASS II DONALD BLAIR MACHUM
PILOT (RCAF), NO. 82 OPERATIONAL TRAINING UNIT
DIED 29TH MAY 1944, AGED 20
BURIED BROOKWOOD MILITARY CEMETERY, UNITED KINGDOM

Tragedy struck on the night of 28/29 May 1944 when a No. 82 Operational Training Unit Wellington, piloted by Donald Machum and returning from a Nickel (leaflet dropping) raid over France, was shot down by a friendly Mosquito fighter. Donald lost his life along with two others in the crew, Leonard Frank Davey and William McGuigan.

The bomb aimer, Boyd Davidson, wrote to his pilot's mother on 11 June.

> Before I start Mrs Machum, let me offer my sincerest sympathies in the loss of your son. I only knew Don for eight weeks, the amount of time we spent flying together at OTU, but I regarded Don as one of my best and truest friends, and his loss to me was like that of a brother. His popularity around the station was unquestionable, and the whole camp was stunned at the news of his death ... We had one of the grandest crews imaginable. Frank Davey, the W.A.G was a great boy; Bill McGuigan, the Tail Gunner was loads of fun. Our old Navigator was fortunate enough to be in the hospital with a bad appendix so he missed the ill-fated trip. The rest of us, Jim Bugley, the Mid-upper, the replacement Navigator and myself, all owe our lives to Don for his cool headedness and great nerve in holding the plane steady as long as he could so we could jump out. We were hit by unidentified aircraft, and the controls were shot away completely. I was sitting beside him in the co-pilot's seat at the time, and immediately we were hit, he grabbed my arm and said 'Jump Davy, I'll hold the kite for you and the crew, get my chute ready, and I'll follow you out'. I jumped at 15,000 feet, and when I left, he was giving instructions to the rest of the crew, and helping them as best he could. In my opinion, when they speak of heroes, I think of Don. It's very few men who will hold the plane and think of the safety of his crew above himself.[181]

Don's commitment and self-sacrifice would subsequently be recognised with the award of a Mention in Despatches.

Donald's brother, Aircraftman 1st Class Ian Machum, lost his life in an accident near Aldergrove, British Columbia, on 16 January 1943, while flying as a passenger in the rear seat of a Harvard. Ian rests in Halifax (Camp Hill) Cemetery.[182]

D. B. MACHUM
ROYAL CANADIAN AIR FORCE
BORN IN HALIFAX, NOVA SCOTIA
OUR DEAR SONS ARE REUNITED
KILLED JANUARY
AND BURIED IN HIS HOME TOWN
PILOT OFFICER
W. H. GEDDES
ROYAL CANADIAN AIR FORCE
SAFE IN THE ARMS OF JESUS

NICE GOING MICHAEL! FAMILY AND FRIENDS PROUD. GOOD LUCK NOW MATE

FLIGHT SERGEANT LOUIS MICHAEL GABRIEL BAKER DFM
AIR GUNNER (RAAF), NO. 166 SQUADRON
DIED 7TH JUNE 1944, AGED 28
BURIED CLICHY NORTHERN CEMETERY, FRANCE

Humour is possibly the last thing one might expect on any epitaph, least of all a wartime epitaph. Yet at least three Bomber Command inscriptions may be considered humorous, and all are Australian.

Michael, as he was known to all, hailed from Toowong in the suburbs of Brisbane, where he was born on 2 October 1915. After leaving school he became a clerk with Brisbane City Electricity Department. By the time he enlisted on 18 July 1942, he was married to Ruth (née Mason) and they had a daughter, Catherine, who had not long turned one.[183]

After embarking for England on 25 May 1943, he went through the usual training units before being posted to No. 166 Squadron based at RAF Kirmington, now Humberside Airport, on 14 November. The crew's first operation was to Berlin and inevitably was a baptism of fire. To quote the ORB:

> It was this crew's first operational sortie, and they had quite an exciting trip… On the way back they strayed off track and were damaged in the port wing and rear turret by flak. They were also attacked by a formation of eight Ju88s which they successfully evaded and beat off. Shortly afterwards they ran into another formation of seven, which again they evaded and beat off, returning and landing safely at base.[184]

Undaunted, they flew another twenty-four ops, including their last: a trip to attack railway targets around Versailles to prevent enemy troop reinforcements reaching the D-Day landing area. By comparison with Berlin, this should have been much less risky but fate dealt them a cruel blow so close to the end of their operational tour. They were shot down by an unknown night fighter and crashed at Saint-Cyr-l'École, west of the target, and all aboard perished.

Michael's DFM was promulgated in *The London Gazette* on 25 January 1946, some 18 months after his death, although with effect from 6 June 1944 – the day before he was killed. The same is true of all seven of the crew. This is unlikely to have been a coincidence. Perhaps their commanding officer, knowing that they were nearing the end of their tour when they would probably have been decorated anyway, and knowing that such awards couldn't be made posthumously, pushed through the recommendations immediately after hearing they had failed to return and before they were presumed dead for official purposes.

GEROEM ZAGINUV U BOYU ZA CANADU I ZA SIMEISTVU SVOYU. TSARSTVO YOMU NEBESNE

PILOT OFFICER NICHOLAS NOVACK
AIR GUNNER (RCAF), NO. 420 (SNOWY OWL) SQUADRON
DIED 29TH JULY 1944, AGED 19
BURIED BECKLINGEN WAR CEMETERY, GERMANY

Translation from Ukrainian:
HE DIED HEROICALLY IN THE BATTLE FOR CANADA
AND FOR HIS FAMILY. THE KINGDOM OF HEAVEN IS HIS.

Nicholas hailed from the greater Edmonton area of Alberta but when he enlisted on 13 January 1943 he was living in Victoria, at the southern tip of Vancouver Island, where he was working as a boilermaker's helper in the shipyards. His assessor described him as 'Well built, wiry, fit. Seems intent, conscientious. Should make aircrew'.[185] His parents, Philip and Eva, were Ukrainian and Nicholas spoke Ukrainian and English fluently.

Nicholas and his crew had been posted to No. 420 Squadron from No. 1666 Heavy Conversion Unit, arriving 4 June 1944.[186] All but the flight engineer were Canadian, a feature typical of Canadian squadrons. Sergeant Unger, the wireless operator, was born in Russia but raised in Canada.[187]

Between 14 June and their last operation beginning 28 July they flew some thirteen sorties – an average of one every three days, although there were occasions when they flew three ops on three consecutive days. The pace must have been as relentless as it was gruelling.

Their fateful flight was to Hamburg and was the first time the city had been on the receiving end of a large attack since the infamous firestorm, exactly one year earlier. This attack was nowhere near as concentrated and most of the damage was to areas already razed in 1943. Nevertheless, more than 17,000 people were evacuated from their homes, many of which would have been temporary wooden shelters after the earlier devastation.[188]

Unfortunately, the night fighters were out in force during the return leg, when bomber streams tended to be much more strung out, making it easier to attack individual bombers. Some 7.2% of the force were lost that night, including Nicholas' Halifax, which was attacked by an unknown night fighter. Four of the crew were able to bail out of the stricken aircraft, although Unger's parachute failed to open and he was found dead a few miles from the crash site. Nicholas' body was found among the wreckage at Estorp, Germany, and initially laid to rest in the local cemetery as an 'unknown airman' before being identified when he was re-interred in 1946.[189]

RUST NOT THE SWORD OF HIS GLORY WITH YOUR TEARS

FLIGHT LIEUTENANT ANTHONY BOWEN LOFTUS TOTTENHAM DFC
PILOT (RAAF), NO. 463 (AUSTRALIAN) SQUADRON
DIED 26TH SEPTEMBER 1944, AGED 21
BURIED WISSANT COMMUNAL CEMETERY, FRANCE

Anthony was the son of Harold William Loftus Tottenham and Veronica Mary Elizabeth Bowen Tottenham (née Perkins), of Mullingar in the Irish Republic.[190] Why then was he enlisted in the Royal Australian Air Force one may wonder?

The Tottenhams were a well-connected society family whose 14,000-acre country seat was Glenfarne Hall in County Leitrim, Ireland, on the banks of Lough MacNean. Anthony's great-grandfather Arthur 'Lofty' Loftus-Tottenham was MP for Leitrim.[191] Many of the extended family served with great distinction during both world wars.

Anthony was born in Kirkwood, north of Port Elizabeth, South Africa on 11 September 1923, although still considered Ireland as the family home. He and his brother Nicholas were visiting their great-uncle in Australia to gain life experience working as jackeroos when their father, a Major with the Royal Norfolk Regiment, was captured by the Japanese during the fall of Singapore in February 1942.[192]

Doubtless motivated by this, both brothers enlisted in Australia shortly afterwards, Anthony in the RAAF and Nicholas in the Australian Pioneers. After completing his training, Anthony was posted to No. 467 Squadron, RAF Waddington, and flew his first operation against Stuttgart on 15/16 March 1944, as second dickie.[193] Towards the end of May, after completing thirteen ops. (including seven aboard the legendary ton-up Lancaster 'S for Sugar', now on display at RAF Museum, Hendon) he was re-assigned to No. 463 Squadron, also at Waddington, where he made another twenty-one trips.[194]

Anthony was awarded a DFC for his actions on the night of 14/15 August, published in *The London Gazette* after his death, the citation for which reads:

> Flying Officer Tottenham has shown himself an able and courageous pilot and captain of aircraft whose many sorties on the most heavily defended and distant targets in Germany have been accomplished with determination and fine airmanship. On one occasion in August, 1944, when detailed to attack a harbour at Brest, his bomb aimer was wounded and the aircraft severely damaged by anti-aircraft fire, but undeterred by the enemy attack, Flying Officer Tottenham completed the mission.

Anthony's fateful operation was a daylight attack against one of the last remaining enemy strongpoints in France, Cap Gris Nez. Shot down by an unknown source, his aircraft crashed at Wissant and the unusually large crew of nine all perished.

AND ALL THE TRUMPETS SOUNDED FOR HIM
ON THE OTHER SIDE

FLIGHT SERGEANT ALAN RAYMOND WILDE
PILOT (RCAF), NO. 24 OPERATIONAL TRAINING UNIT
DIED 13TH OCTOBER 1944, AGED 20
BURIED GOOSE GREEN (ST. PAUL) CHURCHYARD, UNITED KINGDOM

Early in his training, Alan's instructor seemed to like his pupil. 'A keen, sincere lad with good motivation, has sense of humour which made him well liked by his fellow. A good prospect.' Awarded his flying badge in January 1944, Alan travelled from Canada to the UK and arrived at No. 24 Operational Training Unit in September.

On the afternoon of 13 October, returning from a cross-country exercise, Alan was directed to land at RAF Honeybourne, carrying out a second circuit owing to another aircraft on the runway. He then prepared to land and, as the accident report recorded, 'the aircraft lost height steadily, drifting across wind to port until, when quite close to the ground it suddenly turned to starboard and crashed. Fire broke out immediately and all the occupants were killed with the exception of the rear gunner who escaped with slight injuries.' The rear gunner later stated hearing the pilot, during the approach to land, say, 'Who is mucking about with the controls?' and later, 'Crash positions'. Ultimately the accident investigators concluded that the cause of the accident was obscure, but that one of Wellington's engines may have failed on the approach to land, and that there may have been fuel starvation.[195]

Alan had a private funeral, arranged by his aunt, who lived in Wigan. His four colleagues were buried in Brookwood Military Cemetery. In November 1945 Alan's mother Emily wrote to the authorities dealing with Alan's estate, in which she added the following.

> In Memoriam to our son and brother.
> No man could bind him to this earth.
> On sun-tipped wings he loved to fly,
> Away from this confusing world,
> Into the sunny sky.
> He is not lost, our well beloved,
> Nor has he travelled far,
> Just stepped inside Home's loveliest room,
> And left the door ajar.

The choice of epitaph is a line from an oft quoted extract from *The Pilgrim's Progress* by English writer John Bunyan.

> When the day that he must go hence was come, many accompanied him to the riverside, into which as he went, he said, 'Death, where is thy sting?' And as he went down deeper, he said, 'Grave, where is thy victory?' So he passed over, and all the trumpets sounded for him on the other side.

THERE ARE OTHERS, WE KNOW,
BUT HE WAS OURS WE LOVED HIM SO

WARRANT OFFICER DENNIS THOMPSON DFC
AIR BOMBER (RAFVR), NO. 35 (MADRAS PRESIDENCY) SQUADRON
DIED 20TH OCTOBER 1944, AGED 24
BURIED WINTZENBACH PROTESTANT CHURCHYARD, FRANCE

The Commonwealth War Graves Commission record that Dennis' parents Harry and Sybil came from Starbeck, Harrogate and he was married to Lily Thompson. In their choice of epitaph they acknowledge that Dennis was one of so many that were lost, but he was theirs. And a reminder that each and every casualty had their own story, their own loved ones, and the grief following his loss was personal and lasting.

No. 35 Squadron was one of the first Pathfinder squadrons, and it was clear that Dennis, acting as the second air bomber, and his crew of eight were accomplished at their job. Indeed Dennis was already the holder of a Distinguished Flying Cross. A glance through the squadron diary reveals they had been given Deputy Master Bomber duties on some raids prior to 19/20 October attack on Stuttgart, on which they were to act as a 'Visual Centrer'. Taking off in their Avro Lancaster from RAF Graveley at 1756 hours the squadron diarist would later record, 'This aircraft is missing, nothing being heard from it after take off.'[196] The Lancaster crashed at Wintzenbach and the entire crew rests in a row in the village churchyard. In addition to Dennis' epitaph, inscriptions also feature on the headstones of the rest of the crew.

Robert William Brown (Pilot)
GREATER LOVE HATH NO MAN THAN THIS, THAT HE LAY DOWN HIS LIFE

Colin Johnson (Flight Engineer)
ETERNAL REST GIVE UNTO HIM, O LORD;
AND LET PERPETUAL LIGHT SHINE UPON HIM. AMEN

John Anthony Creemer Clarke (Navigator)
WILL ALWAYS BE REMEMBERED.
SPLENDID HE PASSED, THE GREAT SURRENDER MADE

Reginald Francis Jack Bright (Air Bomber)
FOREVER IN OUR THOUGHTS

Adam Linton (Wireless Operator)
AT THE GOING DOWN OF THE SUN AND IN THE MORNING
WE REMEMBER YOU

Frank David Thomas Phillips (Air Gunner)
"PEACE, PERFECT PEACE"
YOUR MEMORY IS HALLOWED IN THE LAND YOU LOVED

Edmond Joseph Kiely (Air Gunner)
ETERNAL REST GRANT UNTO HIM, O LORD;
MAY HE REST IN PEACE. AMEN

HE'S OUTSOARED THE SHADOW OF OUR NIGHT AND LEFT THE VIVID SKIES SIGNED WITH HIS HONOUR

SERGEANT MERVYN LAMBERT TANSLEY
NAVIGATOR (RAFVR), NO. 608 (NORTH RIDING) SQUADRON
DIED 6TH NOVEMBER 1944, AGED 21
BURIED FULHAM PALACE ROAD CEMETERY, UNITED KINGDOM

On 6 November 1944 No. 608 Squadron detailed twelve Mosquitoes for an attack on Gelsenkirchen. The squadron, based at RAF Downham Market, was part of No. 8 Group's Light Night Striking Force, and the raid to Gelsenkirchen would be one of its typical harassing raids, not only inflicting damage but also drawing night fighters away from main force attacks. That night the RAF's heavy bombers would be attacking the Mittelland Canal and Koblenz. Of the twelve Mosquitoes that took off from RAF Downham Market that night, one returned early and another, piloted by James McLean, assisted by navigator Mervyn Tansley, crashed at Bawdeswell, Norfolk.

The suspected cause of the crash was icing, with Mervyn's Mosquito striking power cables before smashing into All Saints Church, which was consumed by the impact and resulting fire. The church was eventually rebuilt and the original tower cross stands to the left of the entrance and inside is a memorial plaque utilising, as a base, some of the Mosquito wreckage. Two houses opposite the church were also badly damaged by flying wreckage, fortunately without any civilian injury.[197]

Mervyn, the son of Fred and Alice Tansley, was buried in his home cemetery in Fulham. James McLean was returned to Scotland and buried in Tranent New Cemetery.

Mervyn's epitaph draws on two sources. This is the second time in this book that a quote from Stephen Spender's *The Truly Great* features (see entry for Stanley Ingle, 27 November 1943), which considers heroism and includes the phrase, 'they travelled a short while toward the sun and left the vivid air signed with their honour.'[198] The first half of Mervyn's epitaph draws upon Percy Bysshe Shelley's poem *Adonais*, written when he was trying to come to terms with the death of poet John Keats. The poem opens with the line 'I weep for Adonais – he is dead!' and includes the following stanza.

> He has outsoared the shadow of our night;
> Envy and calumny and hate and pain,
> And that unrest which men miscall delight,
> Can touch him not and torture not again;
> From the contagion of the world's slow stain
> He is secure, and now can never mourn
> A heart grown cold, a head grown grey in vain;
> Nor, when the spirit's self has ceased to burn,
> With sparkless ashes load an unlamented urn.

SWIFT DEATH AFLAME WITH OFFERING SUPREME AND MIGHTY SACRIFICE

PILOT OFFICER JAMES HEDLEY RICE
WIRELESS OPERATOR (RAFVR), NO. 78 SQUADRON
DIED 21ST NOVEMBER 1944, AGED 34
BURIED ASHBY-DE-LA-ZOUCH CEMETERY, UNITED KINGDOM

The epitaph chosen by James Rice's family comes from a poem by Maurice Baring, who served with the Intelligence Corps during the First World War, attached to the Royal Flying Corps and Royal Air Force. *In Memoriam A.H.* expresses the cherished bond Baring had with an airman, and his grief and emptiness when he is killed, 'Something is broken which we cannot mend'. He recalls his friend's ambition, his 'restless seed', then the sense of foreboding having dreamt 'you were missing'. But then came the 'certain news that you were dead … The fight was fought, and your great task was done.'

> Of all your brave adventures this the last
> The bravest was and best;
> Meet ending to a long embattled past,
> This swift, triumphant, fatal quest,
> Crowned with the wreath that never perisheth,
> And diadem of honourable death;
> Swift Death aflame with offering supreme
> And mighty sacrifice,
> More than all mortal dream;
> A soaring death, and near to Heaven's gate;
> Beneath the very walls of Paradise.

For Baring, his friends name would 'sound for ever in answering halls of fame'. He had 'gained the civic crown of that eternal town' and that his friend was 'Among the chosen few, Among the very brave, the very true'.

The court of inquiry into the loss of James Rice's Halifax recorded, 'The aircraft returning from operations [Sterkrade] was asked to do a dummy run over the flare path to check the visibility. The aircraft flew along the runway at 50-100 ft. climbing only to about 300ft, before commencing to turn. While turning the aircraft lost height and hit some trees 50-60 ft. high two miles from the airfield. The night was very dark and between the time of take off and the crash, the pressure had dropped 6 millibars'. With a total loss of life, the report notes this was the pilot's 'last operational sortie before screening'.[199]

THE ONE GREAT SCORER...
MARKS, NOT THAT YOU WON OR LOST
BUT HOW YOU PLAYED THE GAME

SERGEANT ROBERT EDWARD ERATT
FLIGHT ENGINEER (RAFVR), NO. 419 (MOOSE) SQUADRON
DIED 29TH DECEMBER 1944, AGED 21
BURIED REICHSWALD FOREST WAR CEMETERY, GERMANY

This is the second epitaph in this book drawing upon American sports journalist Grantland Rice quote, 'For when the One Great Scorer comes to write against your name, He marks - not that you won or lost - but how you played the game'. Comparing this epitaph, quoted almost verbatim, to the variation used for Niel Hardy's epitaph (page 42), demonstrates how families adapted quotes, making them specific to their particular loss.

Recorded as initially buried in Gelsenkirchen-Huellen Cemetery, and reburied in Reichswald Forest War Cemetery on 12 May 1947, the graves concentration form of 5 April 1948 noted that Robert was buried in Plot XX Row C Grave 8. However, in February 1950 the mother of pilot Raymond Adam received a letter from the RCAF Casualties Officer, stating.

> You will recall that in our letter of March 1, 1949, you were advised that the members of your son's crew and those of the other crew were resting in plot 20, row C, in the Reichswald Forest British Military Cemetery. Unfortunately your son and one of his crewmates together with two members of the other crew could not be identified separately. Of the four, two could be identified as officers and the other two as Flight Engineers. By elimination one of the officers would be your son and the other officer a member of the other crew. The same situation applies to the Flight Engineers, Sergeant Eratt being the Flight Engineer of your son's crew and the second Flight Engineer being a member of the other crew.
>
> Under the circumstance, therefore, there was no alternative but to register the graves of the two Flight Engineers collectively and to register the graves of the two unidentified officers in like manner. Graves 4 and 5 in row C, plot 20 will be registered collectively with the names of your son and Pilot Officer Maloney of the other crew. Graves 2 and 3 will be registered collectively with the names of your son's Flight Engineer, Sergeant Eratt, and Pilot Officer Feldman the Flight Engineer of the other crew.[200]

Canadian Jacob Feldman, also of 419 Squadron, had also lost his life on the raid to Scholven-Buer on the night of 29/30 December 1944.

CWSG FY MACHGEN HEB DDIHUNO CWSG, A GWYN DY FYD.
DAD, MAM, NELLIE. BANGOR, WALES

SERGEANT RICHARD OSWALD JONES
AIR GUNNER (RAFVR), NO. 102 (CEYLON) SQUADRON
DIED 5TH JANUARY 1945, AGED 21
BURIED HANOVER WAR CEMETERY, GERMANY

The Welsh language elements of the epitaph can be open to different English translations, for example 'May you sleep peacefully my son, may you sleep and be blessed', or 'Sleep unbroken, my boy. Sleep and be blessed'.

Richard was the son of Edison G. and Maggie Jones from Bangor, Wales, and they have drawn upon the poem *Sul y Blodau* by Welsh language poet Eliseus Williams (1867 – 1926), known as 'Eifion Wyn'. Throughout the poem a mother tries to come to terms with, and mourns, the loss of a child, Goronwy Wyn, opening with, "Where the flow'rs and gray stone hide thee, Sleep, my pearl, below".[201] The last stanza of the poem reads as follows.

Slumber yet awhile, Goronwy,	Tan y garreg las, Goronwy,—
Under that gray stone;	Cysga beth yn hwy;
I must say "Good night," Goronwy,	Rhaid yw dweud "Nos da," Goronwy,
Leaving thee alone:	Mynd a'th ado'r wy':
Strange that cradle! hand of mother	Nid oes eisiau llaw i'th siglo
Need not rock thee now:	Yn dy newydd grud;
Sleep until we meet each other,	Cwsg, nes gweld ein gilydd eto,
Sleep, and blest be thou.	Cwsg, a gwyn dy fyd.

On the night of 5/6 January 1945 Bomber Command sent 664 aircraft to attack Hanover, including twenty from No. 102 Squadron. The squadron diarist would subsequently record, 'of this number we were unfortunate enough to lose 3 … Enemy opposition was more severe than of late. Numerous fighter flares were seen on track on the way in from the coast to the target and back again to the coast on the way out.' Richard's Halifax took off at 1652 hours and is believed to have crashed just over two-and-a-half hours later at Frielingen, near Wunstorf, with only one member of the eight-man crew surviving. Those killed were originally buried in Horst Cemetery and then reburied, side by side, in Hanover War Cemetery in October 1946.

SI MONUMENTUM QUAERIS CIRCUMSPICE

FLYING OFFICER JOHN ANDREW SORLEY STEWART
PILOT (RAFVR), NO. 158 SQUADRON
DIED 16TH JANUARY 1945, AGED 23
BURIED BERLIN 1939-1945 WAR CEMETERY, GERMANY

Translation from the Latin
IF YOU SEEK HIS MONUMENT, LOOK AROUND YOU

The epitaph on the tomb of Sir Christopher Wren in St Paul's Cathedral, London, of which he was the architect, reads 'si monumentum requiris, circumspice', translating as 'if you seek his monument, look around'. Anyone reading the epitaph has literally just passed through Wren's 'monument'.

For John Stewart's epitaph, 'quaeris' appears instead of 'requiris'. Both words effectively mean 'to seek', but the request on Wren's epitaph is immediate, referencing the Cathedral itself, whereas John's epitaph invites the reader perhaps to consider the wider legacy of his sacrifice. John's 'monument' is the defeat of Nazism and a free democratic society.

For the raid to Magdeburg on the night of 16/17 January 1945, No. 158 Squadron detailed twenty-three aircraft to take part, although one Handley Page Halifax would return early and another failed to take off when one of the engines caught fire. John Stewart lifted his Halifax from the RAF Lissett runway at 1916 hours, on what would be the crews fourteenth operation. Returning crews told of large fires in the target areas. They also reported flak damage, intense searchlights over Hanover, and seeing other aircraft shot down in flames.[202] Indeed seventeen Halifaxes were lost, including John's which came down near the village of Hordorf. Three of the crew would survive, becoming prisoners-of-war. John lost his life and was initially buried in a collective grave with three of his crew mates in Horsdorf.

All four bodies were exhumed after the war and reburied in the Berlin cemetery on 5 July 1947 – John resting with air gunner Albert Cox (no epitaph), wireless operator Ronald Knight (DEEP IN OUR HEARTS A MEMORY IS KEPT OF ONE WE LOVE AND WILL NEVER FORGET), and air gunner George Yeulett (YOU WILL ALWAYS LIVE IN OUR HEARTS AND MEMORIES. PHYL, BARRI, NEIL AND OUR MUMS).

FORTI NIHIL DIFFICILE

FLIGHT LIEUTENANT BERNARD MATHEW WILLIAMS
PILOT (RAAF), NO. 149 (EAST INDIA) SQUADRON
DIED 5TH MARCH 1945, AGED 19
BURIED REICHSWALD FOREST WAR CEMETERY, GERMANY

Translation from Latin
TO THE BRAVE, NOTHING IS DIFFICULT

Bernard was the son of George and Rose Williams, of Northampton, West Australia, although he gave his married sister Mary Fair as his next of kin when enlisting on 5 December 1942, three months after his eighteenth birthday, since his parents had died in 1940 and 1935 respectively. He had been a surveyor in a local gold mine and also a cadet in the ATC.

On arrival in England in September 1943, he trained with several units before converting to heavy bombers at No. 1660 HCU and finally No. 5 LFS (Lancaster Finishing School). He was then posted operationally to No. 149 Squadron on 8 December 1944, almost exactly two years after enlisting.[203]

Bernard first flew against the enemy on Christmas Eve, 1944. The target was Bonn Hangelar airfield. He didn't fly any second dickie sorties, and at this stage in the war little resistance was forthcoming from the fuel-impoverished Luftwaffe. Indeed, the squadron ORB[204] makes no mention of any fighter activity or anti-aircraft fire and only one aircraft was lost out of a force of 104.

The crews made an early start, taking advantage of the long, dark nights, and were safely back at RAF Methwold in time for last orders at the bar. The unit flew no sorties on Christmas Day or Boxing Day, allowing the men a short respite.

Three months and sixteen operations later, Bernard's fateful operation was to attack the Consolidation benzol plant in Gelsenkirchen, using Gee-H radar owing to complete cloud cover. Two aircraft were lost to flak over the target and five of the airmen aboard Bernard's were able to bail out, becoming prisoners for a short time. Sadly, Bernard was not amongst them.

With neither parent still alive to grieve for him, it is not known who chose his inscription. It may have been his sister Mary. It may possibly have been his school motto, although he moved around a great deal in Western Australia so it is difficult to know.

ONE OF THE BEST.
GUTE NACHT UND GOTT SEI MIT DIR

FLIGHT SERGEANT FRED FEARNLEY
AIR GUNNER (RAFVR), NO. 10 SQUADRON
DIED 5TH MARCH 1945, AGED 39
BURIED DURNBACH WAR CEMETERY, GERMANY

Translation of the German phrase
GOOD NIGHT AND GOD BE WITH YOU

An account of what happened on Fred's Halifax on the fateful night of 5/6 March 1945 is provided by his pilot Dess Moss DFC. Having difficulty releasing a bomb Dess, believing the problem was due to icing, took their aircraft below cloud to warmer air and 'threw the Halifax around a bit'. The bomb eventually fell, and they climbed above the cloud. Fred Fearnley was in the mid under gun position.

> There was a shout from Steve in the rear turret, 'night fighter attacking' and I saw tracers curving away from below and behind us up to starboard. I started corkscrewing as violently as I could, but it was soon obvious that we had been badly hit. The fuselage filled with smoke and I could no longer hear instructions from the rear gunner. Jimmy [the flight engineer] was trying to draw my attention to something and I realised that although we were on fire amidships, the emergency signalling light from the rear gunner was flashing – good for Steve! He kept doing his job and shot down a Ju88. By this time our port inner engine was blazing and out of control, the starboard was also on fire as was the 'rest position' area of the fuselage. I could get no reply from any of the gunners – we had one in the mid-under blister on this trip [Fred] – and we were losing height and unable to bring the flames under control.

Dess ordered his crew to bale out and tapped out the letter 'P' on the emergency signal light, 'in the hope that the gunners would see it and be able to get out in time'. Having seen his flight engineer, with his parachute, make his way to the front escape hatch, Dess found that his seat harness had jammed. He fought to release it, 'and then the world exploded! I woke to find myself dangling in my parachute harness a few feet from the ground.'[205]

Dess was subsequently captured along with two other members of his crew. The five others, including Fred, were originally buried in Babenhausen Civil Cemetery, Germany before being moved to Durnbach in November 1947.

DILEAS GU BAS

FLYING OFFICER DONALD BEATON DSO
PILOT (RAFVR), NO. 514 SQUADRON
DIED 9TH MAY 1945, AGED 22
BURIED CLICHY NORTHERN CEMETERY, FRANCE

Translation from Scots Gaelic
FAITHFUL UNTO DEATH

As the Second World War was nearing its end, and when hostilities in Europe finally ended, tens of thousands of Allied ex-prisoners-of-war needed repatriation. As part of Operation Exodus Bomber Command aircrews played their part. Veterans will often recall this as one of their most rewarding experiences.

Donald Beaton was serving with No. 514 Squadron at the war's end and was already the holder of the Distinguished Service Order, the citation published in *The London Gazette*, 3 November 1944.

> As pilot and captain of aircraft Flying Officer Beaton has completed many operational sorties against a variety of targets in Germany and occupied territory. In September, 1944, he took part in a daylight attack on Le Havre. Whilst over the target the aircraft sustained severe damage when struck by anti-aircraft fire and temporarily went out of control. Flying Officer Beaton was badly wounded, suffering a broken leg and multiple wounds caused by flying fragments of shell. Although in great pain he regained control and set course for home. Making light of his injuries he refused to leave the controls and flew back to an airfield near the coast where he landed his damaged aircraft safely. This officer displayed outstanding courage and fortitude. Though severely wounded he never wavered in his determination to bring his aircraft and its crew home. His example was most inspiring.

Early in May 1945 Donald played his part in Operation Manna, dropping food to the starving Dutch population, then on 9 May, Donald, with five aircrew colleagues, was detailed for an Operation Exodus mission. Having picked up twenty-four ex-POWs at Juvincourt, Donald reported a problem with the controls of his Lancaster, and they would be returning, but the aircraft crashed near Roye-Amy with a total loss of life. Donald, with two of his air force colleagues and nine ex-POW army casualties, now rests in a collective grave in Clichy Northern Cemetery.

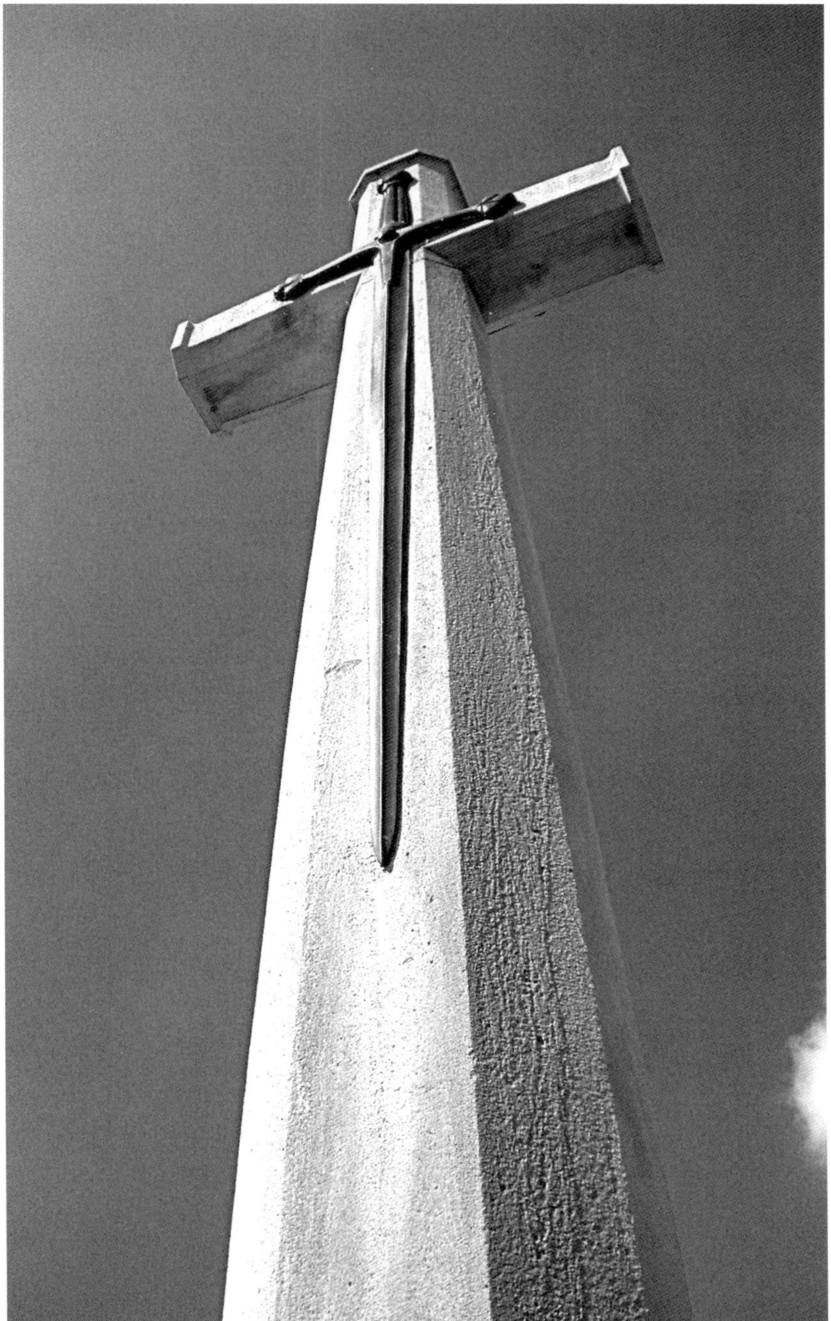

Endnotes

1. The full story of Frederick Oliver and his respective crew is told by Howard Sandall *in V-Weapons Bomber Command Failed to Return* (Fighting High, 2015).
2. The full story of Henry Maudslay is told by Dr Robert Owen in *Henry Maudslay Dam Buster* (Fighting High, 2014).
3. The full story of Jack Fiztgerald and his respective crew is told by Steve Darlow in *Bomber Command Failed to Return* (Fighting High, 2011).
4. Webster, Sir Charles, and Frankland, Noble. *The Strategic Air Offensive Against Germany 1939-1945, Volume IV Annexes and Appendices.* Appendix 40 – Monthly Annual and Grand Totals of Bomber Command Aircraft despatched, missing, and damaged in operations September 1939 to May 1945. The official history notes that 'The following have been excluded: sorties of the Advanced Air Striking Force, Bomber Command anti-submarine patrols, convoy escort duties, minelaying, supply carrying, reconnaissance, anti-invasion exercises and the repatriation of prisoners of war.'
5. The National Archives page https://discovery.nationalarchives.gov.uk/details/r/C16484. Air Ministry: P4 (Cas) Files relating to casualties suffered during air operations and aircraft accidents 1939-1945
6. Statistics from Hadaway, Stuart (January 2021*). Identification methods of the Royal Air Force Missing Research and Enquiry Service, 1944-52.* Forensic Science International. 318. Amsterdam: Elsevier Science, and Gray, Jennie (2016). *Nothing can excuse us if we fail; the British and their dead servicemen, North-West Europe, 1944-1951* (Thesis). Exeter: University of Exeter.
7. https://www.cwgc.org/who-we-are/our-story/the-public-reaction/
8. https://www.cwgc.org/who-we-are/our-story/designing-our-first-war-graves/
9. https://api.parliament.uk/historic-hansard/commons/1920/may/04/imperial-war-graves-commission#S5CV0128P0_19200504_HOC_334
10. Details of Harrogate (Stonefall) Cemetery from the Commonwealth War Graves Commission website www.cwgc.org
11. In the First World War there was, initially, an expectation for relatives to pay for inscriptions, but the various governments were uncomfortable with the policy. Some governments covered the costs if private payment was not received, and others decided not to chase families if payment was not made. In regard the Second World War, Lynelle Howson provided the following explanation. 'In the early months of the Second World War, the IWGC wished to be able to start the process of contacting bereaved families to verify and receive information about their dead of the new war. Having learned from the post First World War issues with requiring private payment, the wording about inscription cost was changed to 'an opportunity' to meet the cost, and 'a contribution' towards the cost of the inscription being welcomed, actual amount to be advised later. To set relatives' expectations regarding the potential contribution, once again an estimate that would not reflect post-war reality was made: 'If borne by relatives the charge will not exceed 7s 6d.' The real costs of engraving headstones had them increase this ceiling figure to £1 in c1945/6. (Correspondence with Lynelle Howson 24 October 2024.)
12. The National Archives No. 107 Squadron Operations Record Books AIR 27/841/3
13. The National Archives AIR 81/1
14. International Bomber Command Centre Losses Database
15. The National Archives. No. 7 Squadron Operations Record Books AIR 27/98/1
16. 'Snaefell Disaster, Isle of Man, 1 January 1940' by Montague Trout – WW2 People's War https://www.bbc.co.uk/history/ww2peopleswar/stories/42/a1071442.shtml
17. The National Archives AIR 81/1764
18. International Bomber Command Centre Losses Database. https://losses.internationalbcc.co.uk/loss/217449

19. The National Archives AIR 81/1980
20. Chorlton, M. *Bomber Command. The Victoria Cross Raids* (Countryside Books, 2014)
21. The National Archives AIR 81/328
22. The National Archives AIR 27/202
23. Commonwealth War Graves Commission
24. 1939 Register
25. The National Archives AIR 27/716
26. With thanks to Selina Joslin, Archivist, Felsted School
27. The National Archives AIR 81/1481
28. The National Archives No. 38 Operations Record Book AIR 27/397/21
29. The National Archives AIR 81/3221
30. The National Archives No. 105 Operations Record Book AIR 27/826/15 and 16
31. The National Archives AIR 81/4238
32. The National Archives No. 115 Operations Record Book AIR 27/887/27 and 28
33. The National Archives AIR 81/4509
34. The National Archives No. 33 Operations Record Book AIR 27/370/37
35. Commonwealth War Graves Commission
36. The National Archives AIR 27/882
37. Barrie, J.M. *Courage - The Rectorial Address Delivered at St. Andrews University, May 3, 1922* (C. Scribner's Sons, 1922)
38. The National Archives AIR 81/6455
39. The National Archives AIR 27/243
40. www.flightsafety.org
41. The National Archives AIR 27/126
42. International Bomber Command Centre Losses Database
43. www.aircrewremembered.com
44. Third Supplement to *The London Gazette*, 8 October 1946
45. The National Archives No. 33 Operations Record Book AIR 27/98/11
46. 1939 Register
47. The National Archives AIR 27/486
48. Boiten, T. *Nachtjagd War Diaries* (Red Kite, 2008)
49. www.yorkshire-aircraft.co.uk
50. Supplement to *The London Gazette*, 9 June 1938
51. 1939 Register
52. Huntingdonshire Cyclist Battalions www.huntscycles.co.uk
53. International Bomber Command Centre Losses Database
54. Ibid
55. Middlebrook, Martin and Everitt, Chris. *The Bomber Command War Diaries* (Midland Publishing Limited, 1996)
56. The National Archives AIR 27/491
57. Boiten, T. *Nachtjagd War Diaries* (Red Kite, 2008)
58. Foreman, Matthews & Parry *Luftwaffe Night Fighter Combat Claims 1939-1945* (Red Kite, 2003)
59. www.the-paulmccartney-project.com/song/war-non-nobis-solum/
60. Wellingborough School website
61. www.natwestgroupremembers.com/our-fallen/our-fallen-ww2.html
62. International Bomber Command Centre Losses Database
63. The National Archives AIR 81/9107
64. The National Archives AIR 81/9186
65. The National Archives AIR 27/821
66. https://public-domain-poetry.com/william-arthur-dunkerley/christs-all-28226
67. The National Archives AIR 81/9367
68. International Bomber Command Centre Losses Database
69. The National Archives AIR 81/10869
70. The National Archives AIR 27/655
71. Middlebrook, Martin and Everitt, Chris. *The Bomber Command War Diaries* (Midland Publishing Limited, 1996)
72. Robb, Reginald Francis. Second World War Service Files – War Dead, 1939 to 1947. Reference:RG 24, Volume 28526. Library and Archives Canada
73. The National Archives AIR27/1048
74. www.yorkshire-aircraft.co.uk
75. I am grateful to Iain MacGillivray for help with this translation, stating 'Idiomatic expressions are always a bit opaque (in any language) but my take, first a bit literally, is 'Your choice of path/journey was as you died', or 'You chose your path/journey as you died'. (Where 'cuairt' - path/journey, even a wander or walk - is being used to mean 'life'). And thus in a bit more proper, but now itself quite idiomatic, opaque English, the

sense is 'You lived as you died', but could also have a sense of, "You died doing what you wanted/loved'. I think the sense in both is someone who lived their lives. Made their choices boldly and freely.'

76. Bowman, Martin. *The Reich Intruders: RAF Light Bomber Raids in World War II* (Pen and Sword Aviation, 2019)
77. The National Archives AIR 81/12549
78. The National Archives AIR 27/1319
79. Middlebrook, Martin and Everitt, Chris. *The Bomber Command War Diaries* (Midland Publishing Limited, 1996)
80. Tyler, William Stone. Second World War Service Files – War Dead, 1939 to 1947. Reference:RG 24, Volume 28846. Library and Archives Canada
81. The National Archives AIR 81/13462
82. https://www.invisibleworks.co.uk
83. Bain, John Douglas Norman. Second World War Service Files – War Dead, 1939 to 1947. Reference:RG 24, Volume 24783. Library and Archives Canada
84. Housman, A.E. *A Shropshire Lad*
85. The National Archives AIR 27/814
86. Commonwealth War Graves Commission
87. From page 5 of *The Mail*, 6 February 1918, sourced via www.findmypast.co.uk
88. The National Archives AIR 81/14925
89. Pilborough, William Edgar. Second World War Service Files – War Dead, 1939 to 1947. Reference:RG 24, Volume 28429. Library and Archives Canada
90. The National Archives. No. 35 Squadron Operations Record Books AIR 27/379/30, AIR 27/379/31, AIR 27/379/32, AIR 27/379/33
91. The National Archives AIR 27/1787
92. Ancestry website
93. Clutton-Brock, Oliver, *Footprints on the Sands of Time* (Grub Street, 2003)
94. With thanks to Jane Gilbert, Canada for invaluable assistance in researching the Jefferies family
95. The National Archives Air 27/1002
96. Boiten, T. *Nachtjagd War Diaries* (Red Kite, 2008)
97. Clutton-Brock, Oliver, *Footprints on the Sands of Time* (Grub Street, 2003)
98. International Bomber Command Centre Losses Database
99. The National Archives. No. 44 Squadron Operations Record Books AIR 27/449/12
100. https://www.uboat.net/allies/merchants/crews/ship2496.html
101. Templeton, Pat Neff, Second World War Service Files – War Dead, 1939 to 1947. Reference:RG 24, Volume: 28789. Library and Archives Canada
102. International Bomber Command Centre Losses Database
103. The National Archives. No. 460 Squadron Operations Record Books AIR 27/1907/11
104. *The London Gazette*, 26 July 1918
105. *The London Gazette*, 11 December 1917
106. With thanks to Alex Browne, College Archivist, Trinity Hall, Cambridge.
107. The National Archives AIR 27/126
108. The National Archives AIR27/973
109. International Bomber Command Centre Losses Database
110. UK BMD records
111. Commonwealth War Graves Commission
112. www.findagrave.com/memorial/158540206/robert_macdonald
113. The ORB (The National Archives AIR 27/487). Note that this document incorrectly states that Flight Sergeant D.A. MacDonald was aboard. There may be other instances where this holds true, so he may have flown more than 8 operations.
114. RAAF Personnel file, National Archives of Australia: A9301, 405576
115. The National Archives AIR 27/371
116. Middlebrook, Martin and Everitt, Chris. *The Bomber Command War Diaries* (Midland Publishing Limited, 1996)
117. Boiten, T. *Nachtjagd War Diaries* (Red Kite, 2008)
118. International Bomber Command Centre Memorials Database
119. International Bomber Command Centre Losses Database
120. UK BMD Records
121. https://internationalbcc.co.uk/about-ibcc/news/sgt-grey-cumberbatch/
122. https://forum.rafcommands.com/forum/general-category/6858-george-medal-to-graham-george-williams#post149822
123. https://www.rafweb.org/Awards/GM_Holders2.htm
124. Grainger, James George. Second World War Service Files – War Dead, 1939 to 1947. Reference:RG 24, Volume 27627. Library and Archives Canada
125. The National Archives. No. 102 Squadron Operations Record Books AIR 27/809/8
126. RAAF Personnel file, National Archives of Australia: A9301, 413329

127. Lambert, Max, *Night after Night: New Zealanders in Bomber Command* (HarperCollins, 2005)
128. International Bomber Command Centre Losses Database
129. Chorley, W.R. *RAF Bomber Command Losses of the Second World War* series (Midland Publishing)
130. Clutton-Brock, Oliver, *Footprints on the Sands of Time* (Grub Street, 2003)
131. The National Archives. No. 158 Squadron Operations Record Books AIR 27/1048/33
132. International Bomber Command Centre Losses Database
133. The National Archives AIR 27/1351
134. Boiten, T. *Nachtjagd War Diaries* (Red Kite, 2008)
135. www.danishww2pilots.dk
136. Boiten, T. *Nachtjagd War Diaries* (Red Kite, 2008)
137. Hinchliffe, Peter. *Schnaufer: Ace of Diamonds* (Tempus, 1999)
138. The National Archives AIR 27/646
139. Supplement to *The London Gazette*, 4 May 1943
140. Holm & Buchner, *A Place of Honour – Manitoba's War Dead Commemorated in its Geography* (Manitoba Conservation, 2005)
141. Laberge, Joseph Claude Albert. Second World War Service Files – War Dead, 1939 to 1947. Reference:RG 24, Volume 27930. Library and Archives Canada
142. Macintyre, John Scott. Second World War Service Files – War Dead, 1939 to 1947. Reference:RG 24, Volume 28072. Library and Archives Canada
143. The National Archives. No. 51 Squadron Operations Record Books AIR 27/492/32
144. Stichting Beeldbank Historisch Bergen. www.beeldbankbergen.nl/cgi-bin/wargraves.pl
145. The National Archives AIR 27/1852
146. Supplement to *The London Gazette*, 10 September 1943
147. Commonwealth War Graves Commission
148. National Archives of Australia. NAA: A9300, HOOD R T
149. Foderingham, Clifford. Second World War Service Files – War Dead, 1939 to 1947. Reference:RG 24, Volume 27521. Library and Archives Canada
150. RAAF Personnel file, National Archives of Australia: A9301, 423710
151. International Bomber Command Centre Memorials Database
152. The National Archives AIR 27/100
153. Boiten, T. *Nachtjagd War Diaries* (Red Kite, 2008)
154. UK BMD Register
155. The National Archives AIR 27/1048
156. Middlebrook, Martin and Everitt, Chris. *The Bomber Command War Diaries* (Midland Publishing Limited, 1996)
157. The National Archives. No. 83 Squadron Operations Record Books AIR 27/687/15 to 22
158. Vennes, Joseph Jules Jean Jacques. Second World War Service Files – War Dead, 1939 to 1947. Reference:RG 24, Volume 28863. Library and Archives Canada
159. https://gutenberg.org/cache/epub/15033/pg15033-images.html
160. *CHESS* (published in Sutton Coldfield), Volume 9, Issue No.102, March 1944, page 85
161. With thanks to Will Radford, Sutton Valance School for his research
162. International Bomber Command Centre Losses Database
163. Commonwealth War Graves Commission
164. www.cementeriobritanico.org.ar/Roll-of-Honour-WWII-1939-1945.pdf
165. Stephen Spender, 'The Truly Great' from *Collected Poems 1928-1953*. (Ed Victor Ltd)
166. The National Archives. No. 460 RAAF Squadron Operations Record Books AIR 27/1908/21-24
167. Mitchell, Henry Osmond. Second World War Service Files – War Dead, 1939 to 1947. Reference:RG 24, Volume 28256. Library and Archives Canada
168. Baroni, Raymond John. Second World War Service Files – War Dead, 1939 to 1947. Reference:RG 24, Volume 24805. Library and Archives Canada
169. http://www.grimsbytelegraph.co.uk/Remembering-youngest-bomber-squadron-commanding/story-14269230-detail/story.html
170. https://www.northlincsweb.net/103Sqn/html/david_holford_dso_dfc.html
171. Dr Theo Boiten, author of the *Nachtjagd War Diaries* (Red Kite, 2008), describes the incident in https://forum.rafcommands.com/forum/general-category/14642-156-sqn-lancaster-ja674-lost-20-21-12-1943#post150000
172. International Bomber Command Centre Losses Database https://losses.internationalbcc.co.uk/loss/228606
173. The Old Eagle House Society website archive http://web.archive.org/web/20160308080741/http://oehs.org.uk/aircrash.html
174. Hjartarson, Frederick Jacob. Second World War Service Files – War Dead, 1939 to 1947. Reference:RG 24, Volume 27741. Library and Archives Canada
175. Little, Martin Stewart. Second World War Service Files – War Dead, 1939 to 1947. Reference:RG 24, Volume 28004. Library and Archives Canada

176. The Project Gutenberg EBook of Rubaiyat of Omar Khayyam, by Omar Khayyam. https://www.gutenberg.org/files/246/246-h/246-h.htm
177. RAAF Personnel file, National Archives of Australia: A9300, PINN G P, 5252225
178. The National Archives AIR 27/1926
179. Roach, Fred. Second World War Service Files – War Dead, 1939 to 1947. Reference:RG 24, Volume 28525. Library and Archives Canada
180. https://www.bombercommandmuseumarchives.ca/s/halifaxlw682.html
181. Machum, Donald Blair. Second World War Service Files – War Dead, 1939 to 1947. Reference:RG 24, Volume 28144. Library and Archives Canada
182. Machum, Ian Thompson. Second World War Service Files – War Dead, 1939 to 1947. Reference:RG 24, Volume 28144. Library and Archives Canada
183. RAAF Personnel file, National Archives of Australia: A9301, 426507
184. The National Archives AIR 27/1089
185. Novack, Nicholas. Second World War Service Files – War Dead, 1939 to 1947. Reference:RG 24, Volume 28345. Library and Archives Canada
186. The National Archives AIR 27/1826
187. Canadian Virtual War Memorial
188. Middlebrook, Martin and Everitt, Chris. *The Bomber Command War Diaries* (Midland Publishing Limited, 1996)
189. Commonwealth War Graves Commission
190. Commonwealth War Graves Commission
191. www.wikitree.com
192. vwma.org.au
193. The National Archives AIR 27/1931
194. The National Archives AIR 27/1921
195. Wilde, Alan Raymond. Second World War Service Files – War Dead, 1939 to 1947. Reference:RG 24, Volume 191982. Library and Archives Canada
196. The National Archives. No. 35 Squadron Operations Record Books AIR 27/381/20
197. Further details of the crash including photographs can be found via https://bawdeswell.net/rtwebsite/villages/Bawdeswell/Baw%20Ch/Mosquito.htm and https://aviationtrails.wordpress.com/2019/11/06/mosquito-crew-p-o-james-mclean-and-sgt-mervyn-tansley-rafvr/
198. Stephen Spender, 'The Truly Great' from *Collected Poems 1928-1953*. (Ed Victor Ltd)
199. Robertson, Wilbert James. Second World War Service Files – War Dead, 1939 to 1947. Reference:RG 24, Volume 28536. Library and Archives Canada
200. Adam, Raymond Francis. Second World War Service Files – War Dead, 1939 to 1947. Reference:RG 24, Volume 24716. Library and Archives Canada
201. Translations by J.W. Wynne-Jones, M.A. https://cy.wikisource.org/wiki/Telynegion_Maes_a_M%C3%B4r_(Testun_Cyfansawdd)
202. The National Archives AIR 27/1050/8
203. RAAF Personnel file, National Archives of Australia: A9300, WILLIAMS B M, 5241304
204. The National Archives AIR 27/1004
205. Dess Moss's full account of what happed that night can be found on https://aircrewremembered.com/moss-dess.html

Acknowledgements

We are sincerely grateful to Lynelle Howson, Historian at the Commonwealth War Graves Commission, and Stuart Hadaway, Research and Information Manager at the Air Historical Branch, for casting their eye over the introduction to the book and offering clarity and suggestions. Appreciation also extends to Simon Bendry, Trevor Bishop, Dan Ellin, Iain MacGillivray, David Mole, Phil Nixon, John Saunders, and Kelvin T. Youngs (aircrewremembered.com).

Dave extends special thanks to his son Joe Gilbert for his expert proof-reading and suggestions, to his cousin Jane Gilbert of Canada for her help with the genealogy of the Canadian entries, but most of all to his wife, who is confusingly also called Jane Gilbert, for putting up with it all.

Sincere thanks also to the team of volunteers who, together with Dave, recorded the epitaphs for inclusion in the Losses Database: Alan Abbey, Andy Hamilton, Anna Hutchesson, Anne Newcombe, Anne Pickersgill, Bob Lindsay, Carol Allen, Chris Jones, Chris Merriman, Di Ablewhite, Dick Swallow, Graham Kent, Jan Hall, Jane McLean, Jill Alder, Jimmy Tarbox (sadly no longer with us), John Babington, Jordan Richardson-Smith, Katie Gilbert, Kevan Chippendale, Liz Prissick, Marie Haynes-Perks, Mark Condron, Mark Hanson, Michelle Rhodes, Mike Connock, Mike Dunlop, Nikki Jones, Robert Taylor, Steve Baldwin, Tony Emptage, Tony Hibberd, and Emily Hibberd.

Picture Credits

Steve Darlow/Fighting High, pages xi, xix, 3, 6, 19, 26, 48, 49, 64, 85, 88, 96, 110, 117. International Bomber Command Centre Digital Archive, Losses Database, pages xvi and xvii (David Leitch original donor, https://ibccdigitalarchive.lincoln.ac.uk/omeka/collections/document/31226), and 20, 21, 66, 86. The National Archives, pages 12, 34, 35. Photo collection of the Danish National Museum, page 61. Library and Archives Canada, pages 87, 95. Cheltenham College, page 48. Tim Laye of Newmarket, Ontario, Canada for the photo of Reg Robb's plaque, page 32. Operation:PictureMe, page 109.

Glossary

Abbreviations
a/c	Aircraft
AFC	Air Force Cross
ATC	Air Training Corps.
BEM	British Empire Medal
DFC	Distinguished Flying Cross
DFM	Distinguished Flying Medal
HCU	Heavy Conversion Unit
IBCC	International Bomber Command Centre, Lincoln
IFF	Identify Friend or Foe
LFS	Lancaster Finishing School
MC	Military Cross
MiD	Mention in Despatches
MRES	Missing Research and Enquiry Service
MREU	Missing Research and Enquiry Unit
NJG	Nachtjagdgeschwader (German: Night Fighter Wing)
OC	Officer Commanding
Op.	Operational sortie
ORB	Operations Record Book
OTU	Operational Training Unit
RAAF	Royal Australian Air Force
RAF	Royal Air Force
RAFVR	Royal Air Force Volunteer Reserve
RCAF	Royal Canadian Air Force
S/L	Searchlights
VC	Victoria Cross

Terms	
Second Dickie	The custom of newly graduated pilots flying one or two operations with a more senior pilot to gain air experience before becoming captain of their own aircraft.
Ace in a day	A fighter pilot achieving five or more victories in a single day.
Grave Concentration	The practice of moving graves from small, remote churchyard and cemeteries to large Commonwealth War Graves Commission cemeteries, where they could be more easily maintained in perpetuity.
Ton-Up	An aircraft that has flown at least 100 operational sorties.
Gee-H	Transponder based navigational system.
Other Ranks	Non-commissioned personnel.
Circus	Operations involving modest numbers of bombers, escorted by fighters, to entice enemy fighters into combat.
Geodetic/Geodesic	Lattice style airframe construction used on several Vickers aircraft, notably the Wellington, and known for its strength due to its use of an inter-connected triangular framework.
Wimpy	Wellington Bomber.
Screening	The practice of removing an airman from operations, having completed a prerequisite number. Some were given desk jobs whilst others became instructors in training units.
Monica	Radar equipment placed at the rear of the aircraft to warn of approaching fighters. Withdrawn mid-1944 after it was discovered that German night-fighters were equipped with equipment to detect the radar, allowing them to locate the bombers from the very equipment designed to defend them.
Nickel	Operations in which propaganda leaflets were dropped over enemy or occupied territory from bombers.

Index

1 MREU 7
1 PRU 5
1 Signals School 42
2 Group 12
2 MREU 11, 70
II./NJG1 59
3 Group 11
3 Recruiting Centre 42
4 EFTS 63
4./NJG 1 20
4 MREU 81
5 Holland Section MREU 37
5 Group 52
5 LFS 107
6./NJG 2 43
7 Bombing and Gunnery School 40
7 EFTS 35
7 Squadron 4, 19, 71
8 Group 94, 102
9 Squadron 18, 23, 47, 54, 70, 81, 90
10 OTU 54
10 Squadron 108
12./NJG 1 71
12 OTU 85
12 Squadron 94
14 OTU 42, 53
15 (B) Squadron 8, 54, 57
15 OTU 52, 69
16 OTU 68, 77, 80
17 OTU 21, 68
18 (Burma) Squadron 17, 24
19 OTU 40
20 OTU 16
22 OTU 45, 66
23 OTU 47, 74
24 OTU 100
25 OTU 51
27 OTU 67
28 OTU 50
33 Squadron 33
35 Squadron 35, 40, 101
38 Squadron 11
42 OTU 14
44 Squadron 44, 52
49th American Station Hospital 92
50 Squadron ix, 20, 42, 51
51 OTU 54

51 Squadron 22, 65
53rd Battalion 68
57 Squadron 29, 30
58 Squadron 15, 25
74 Graves Concentration Unit 1
75 Squadron 60, 62
76 Squadron 89
77 Squadron 28, 31
78 Squadron 103
82 OTU 95
83 Squadron 73
88 Squadron 9
100 Squadron 54, 82
101 Squadron 55, 76
102 Squadron 10, 55, 105
103 Squadron 38, 54, 78, 83, 84
104 Squadron 27
105 Squadron 12
106 Squadron 75
107 Squadron 1, 85
110 Squadron 1
114 Squadron 14
115 Squadron 13
142 Squadron 47
144 Squadron ix, 2
149 Squadron 39, 43, 107
150 Squadron 7, 36
156 Squadron 37, 67
158 Squadron 32, 58, 72, 106
166 Squadron 97
214 Squadron 34
218 Squadron 59, 61
226 Squadron 5, 33
405 Squadron xvii, 35, 41
419 Squadron 104
420 Squadron 98
426 Squadron 92
428 Squadron 78
429 Squadron 63, 66, 92
460 Squadron 46, 67, 79
463 Squadron 99
466 Squadron 91
467 Squadron 99
514 Squadron 109
608 Squadron 102
611 Squadron 23
617 Squadron 52
619 Squadron 81

622 Squadron xiii
692 Squadron 94
1503 Beam Approach Training Flight 43
1652 Conversion Unit 40
1656 Heavy Conversion Unit 86
1658 Conversion Unit 56
1659 Heavy Conversion Unit 87
1660 Heavy Conversion Unit 107
1661 Conversion Flight 52
1663 Heavy Conversion Unit 72
1666 Heavy Conversion Unit 98
Stab I./NJG1 61
Stab IV./NJG1 52

Aachen 47
Abercromby, Flight Lieutenant 51
Adam, Raymond 104
AG Weser 43
Air Ministry xiv, 1, 28, 39, 42
Aldergrove 95
Alexander, Dorothy 43
Alexander, George 43
Alexander, Georgina 43
Alexander, Michael 43
Allen, John 63
Allen, Richard 11
Amifontaine 6
Antwerp 12
Aptroot, Flight Lieutenant 7
Arkwright, John 8,62
Arlberg 10
Arnold Cemetery 19
Arnold, Roy 18
Ashy-de-la-Zouch Cemetery 103
Aylesbury 17

Babenhausen Civil Cemetery 108
Bærum 80
Bailey, Albert 94
Bailey, Arthur 70
Bailey, Dorothy 94
Bailey, Frances 94
Bailey, Francis 70
Bailey, Mary 70
Bailey, Sydney 94

Baker, Catherine 97
Baker, Ernest 17
Baker, Louis 97
Baker, Ruth 97
Baldwin, Stanley 2
Balestier, Caroline 89
Balestier, Wolcott 89
Balliol Chapel 76
Bank of New South Wales 57
Bannan, J.R. 69
Baring, Maurice 103
Barkel, Albert 50
Barmby-on-the-Moor (St. Catherine) Churchyard 32
Barnes, Elizabeth 5
Barnes, William 43
Baroni, Marie 81
Baroni, Michael 81
Baroni, Raymond 81
Barrie, James 16
Barth 89
Basingstoke (Worting Road) Cemetery 5
Bata Shoe Company 32
Bath (Haycombe) Cemetery 86
Bath 36, 86
Bawdeswell 102
Bax, Tom 18
Beaconsfield Cemetery 69
Beaton, Donald 109
Beauvais 33
Beck, Howard 56
Becklingen War Cemetery 42, 98
Beech Hill xiii
Belgian Aviation History Association 92
Bennett, Keith 46
Bentz, Wilbur 92
Berck-sur-Mer 14
Bergen General Cemetery 65
Bergen-op-Zoom Canadian War Cemetery 14, 37, 65
Bergen-op-Zoom Cemetery 37
Berlin 1939–1945 War Cemetery 6, 25, 26, 73, 79, 81
Berlin xvii, 33, 42, 57, 73, 75, 76, 78, 79, 81, 82, 97
Bethell, Kathleen 87
Bicester Cemetery 45
Binyon, Laurence 16, 94
Bishop, Billy 45
Bland, Aircraftman 55
Blankenberge Communal Cemetery 18
Bolsward 43
Bomber Command Memorial 4, 92
Bomber Command Museum of Canada 92
Bondi Bay 57
Bonenfant, Joseph 63
Bonn 107
Boon, John 7
Bordeaux 13
Bötel, Hans-Georg 43
Bottisham xviii
Boulogne 12

Bowman, Martin 33
Bradford (Scholemoor) Cemetery 69
Branton, Ida 5
Branton, Jacob 5
Branton, John 5
Branton, John (junior) 5
Branton, Lydia 5
Branton, William 5
Bremen 20, 40, 42, 43, 52
Brenchley (All Saints) Churchyard 30
Brest 15, 47, 99
Brighouse Cemetery 16
Bright, Reginald 101
Brightmore, Ted 4
Brisbane 42, 97
Brissenden, Joseph 16
Bristol 2
Britton, D.N. 73
Brookwood Military Cemetery xvi, 51, 54, 87, 95, 100
Brown, Robert 101
Bruce, Dominic 18
Bruehl 35
Brussels 12
Brussels Town Cemetery 12
Brusthem (St Trond) Cemetery 60
Buckingham Palace 66
Buenos Aires 47, 77
Bunyan, John 100
Burns, Robert 69
Burnett, Wing Commander 22
Burton, Dorothy 77
Burton, John 77
Burton, William 77
Burton-on-the-Wolds Burial Ground 50
Butler, Vernon 33
Butterworth, George 38
Byron Bay 52

Cambridge 77
Cambridge City Cemetery xvii, xix, 9, 47, 67, 77, 82
Cambridge University 47
Campbell, Thomas 25
Canterbury 36
Cap Griz Nez 99
Cardiff 65
Cardinal Vaughan Memorial School 6
Carlisle (Dalston Road) Cemetery 53
Carlisle 53
Carter, Edwin Roland 30
Carter, Edwin 71
Castricum Protestant Churchyard 65
Cefn-y-strad 13
Chamberlain, Neville 91
Chapman, Paul 8
Chateauquay Basin 40
Chatteris 21
Cheltenham College 47

Cherbourg 41
Chippenham 15
Chislehurst Cemetery 30
Choloy War Cemetery 9
Chorley Wood 87
Chorley, William 33
Churchill, Winston xv
Churn, T. 69
Cicero 23
Clarke, John 101
Clement, Henry 55
Clement, Mary 55
Clement, William 55
Clichy Northern Cemetery 97, 109
Cliftonville 77
Coates, Annie 14
Coates, Jack 14
Coates, John 14
Colbourn, Cecil 8
Colbourn, Charles 8
Colbourn, Gertrude 8
Colbourn, Jean 8
Coleby Grange 75
Colditz 18
Cole, John 65
Colline-Beaumont 91
Collins, Francis
Collins, Leonard 43
Cologne (Köln) 20, 37, 38, 41, 47
Commonwealth War Graves Commission 1,5, 23, 53, 74, 84, 85, 101
Copenhagen 61
Cormack, John 35
Cormack, W.T. 37
Cornwell, Herbert xviii
Côte-des-Neiges 41
Cottier, Mrs 4
Cown, Nick 87
Cox, Albert 106
Creamer, K.T. 69
Cuke, Mark 54
Culworth 77
Cumberbatch, Charles 54
Cumberbatch, Grey 54
Cumberbatch, Octavia 54
Cuxhaven 65

Darby, Robert 70
Davey, Leonard 95
Davidson, Boyd 95
Davidstow Moor 86
Davies, Percy 5
De More 14
Dearmer, Percy 24
Dening, John 52
Denton Holme 53
Diddington 94
Dieghem 12
Diss 80
Dixon, Daniel 34
Dixon, Eric 34
Dixon, Evelyn 34
Doeberitz 73
Don Valley 21

Dortmund 35, 59
Dorval 63
Douzy Communal Cemetery 7
Dresden 59
Du Mont, Mr 76
Dufton, charles 11
Duisberg 39, 56
Dukinfield Cemetery 30
Dunkerley, William 28
Dunkley, Ronald 28
Dunlop, Andrew 54
Dunn, W.A. 5
Dunville 32
Durban 44
Durham Light Infantry 38
Durnbach War Cemetery 70, 75, 76, 83, 108
Düsseldorf xviii, 22, 31, 39, 44, 46, 51, 57, 60, 94

Eagle House School 85
East Finchley 6
East Wretham 30
Easterlow, Bernard 90
Edmonds, John 39
Edmonton 98
Eindhoven (Woensel) General Cemetery 22
Eindhoven 22
Elliott, Joseph 53
Ellis, Alice 13
Ellis, Hylton 13
Ellis, William 13
Emden 40
Emerson, Ralph 2
Empress of Canada 81
England, Charles 39
England, Dennis 39
England, Louisa 39
England, Olive 39
English Social Club 77
Epping 91
Eratt, Robert 104
Esbjerg (Fourfelt) Cemetery 56
Essen 39, 40, 41, 58, 65
Eston 5
Estorp 98
Eupen 59
Evitt, Henry 9
Evitt, Susannah 9
Exeter 36
Exeter Higher Cemetery 27

Fair, Mary 107
Falmouth 47
Fearnley, Fred 108
Feldman, Jacob 104
Felsted Independent School 9
Feltwell (St. Nicholas) Churchyard 30
Fidell, Edith 19
Fidell, Ernest 19
Fidell, James 19
Finlay, Charles 72

Finlay, Elizabeth 72
Finlay, George 72
Finow Cemetery 81
FitzGerald, Edward 90
Fitzgerald, Jack xiii, xv, xviii
Flem-Moor 28
Floersbach Civil Cemetery 83
Flushing)Vlissingen) Northern Cemetery 47
Foderingham, Clifford 67
Foley, William 56
Ford 17
Fortune, Thomas 7
Frankfurt 22, 62
Frankfurt Main Cemetery 76
Frazer, Clive 68
Frazer, Jack 68
Fredericia 61
Frielingen 105
Frost, Robert 31
Fulham Palace Road Cemetery 102

Gallipoli 75
Gammell Rye Churchyard xviii
Garai, Earle 59
Garland, Donald 6, 8
Garland, Patrick 6
Garland, Winifred 6
Garner, Wing Commander xi
Garrett, Fydell 75
Gavin, Anne 12
Gavin, Charles 12
Gee, Delphine 50
Gee, Donald 50
Gee, Leslie 50
Gelsenkirchen 102, 107
Gelsenkirchen-Huellen Cemetery 104
Geraardsbergen Communal Cemetery 92
Gieten General Cemetery 71
Gilze-Rijen 14
Glanfarne Hall 99
Glasgow 80
Glasspool Charity Trust 39
Gneisnau 82
Godwin College 77
Goose Green (St. Paul) Churchyard 100
Gordon, Harold 15
Görlitz 89
Goudswaard 72
Grantham 53
Gray, Thomas 6
Greig, Nordhal 79
Grimsby (Scartho Road) Cemetery 69
Groningen 20
Gross-Karben 75
Guest, Jack 20
Gurd, Philip 30

Hadsund 61
Haines, George 22

Haines, James 22
Haines, Mary 22
Halifax (Camp Hill) Cemetery 95
Hamburg 59, 67, 98
Hammersmith 29
Hammond, Jay 92
Hanau 34
Hancock, Peter 83
Hangelar airfield 107
Hanover 52, 72, 105
Hanover War Cemetery 54, 105
Hardenhuish (St. Nicholas) Churchyard) 15
Hardewijk General Cemetery 54
Hardy, Niel 42
Hardy, Olive 42
Harich 52
Harris, Arthur 34, 50
Harris, Charles 8
Harris, Cyril 17
Harrison, George 23
Harrogate (Stonefall) Cemetery xvii, 69, 78
Harrogate 101
Harrow (Pinner) Cemetery 4
Harvey, Alan 35
Haslum Cemetery 80
Hasselt 91
Headland, Bertram 16
Heeze 22
Heligoland Bight ix, 2
Helvard, Angla 61
Helvard, Arne 61
Helvard, Jens 61
Hemans, Felicia 60
Henderson, Thomas 84
Hendon 99
Heverlee War Cemetery 6, 40, 54, 58, 60
Heyes, Elizabeth 66
Heyes, Thomas (junior) 66
Heyes, Thomas 66
Hill, W.G. 66
Hilton, Wing Commander 73
Hilts, John 28
Hitler, Adolf 91
Hjartarson, Frederick 86
Hjartarson, Ivar 86
Hjartarson, Rosa 86
HMS Begum 5
Hoboken, Jacques 75
Hobro 61
Holford, David 82
Holford, Jean 82
Hood, Robert 67
Hordorf 106
Horst Cemetery 105
Hotel Hamilton 81
Hotton War Cemetery 59
Housman, Alfred 38
Howell, James 25
Howell, Kathleen 25
Howells, Owen 1
Hughes, Edward 16
Humberside Airport 97

Ijmuiden 65
Imperial War Graves Commission xv, xvi, xviii, 1, 9,12, 13, 19, 80, 86
Ingle, Stanley 78
International Bomber Command Centre ix, x, 31, 62, 84
International Red Cross xiv, 11, 31, 42, 56
Isle of Man 4

Jackson, Stanley 30
Jacobovitch, Anne 20
Jacobovitch, Isaac 20
Jacobovitch, Israel 20
Jacobovitch, Jack 20
Jacobovitch, Miriam 20
James, Eric 11
Jefferies, Ernest (junior) 41
Jefferies, Ernest 41
Jefferies, Ruby 41
Jefferies, Walter 41
Jenkins, James 75
Jersey 30
Johannesburg 20
Johnson, Colin 101
Johnston, Henry 23
Johnston, Kathleen 23
Johnston, Robert 23
Johnston, Robert 23
Johnstone, James 11
Jones, Edison 105
Jones, Leslie 50
Jones, Maggie 105
Jones, Malcolm 35
Jones, Richard 105
Jonkerbos War Cemetery 52, 57
Juvincourt 109

Kassel 72, 75
Keats, John 102
Kelstern 82
Kempston Cemetery 54
Kenninghall 67
Kew (Melbourne) 68
Khayyam, Omar 90
Kiechlinsbergen 70
Kiel 23, 32
Kiel War Cemetery 13, 28
Kiely, Edmond 101
King, Charles 54
King, Harold 16
King, Lorna 71
Kipling, Rudyard 89
Kirk, Thomas 82
Kirkwood 99
Kjarsgaard, Karl 92
Klagenfurt War Cemetery 10
Knight, Clayton 45
Knight, Ronald 106
Koblenz 102
Krefeld 61

Laberge, Eugene 63
Laberge, Helen 63
Laberge, Joseph 63
Lamsdorf 43
Lanaken 6
Landrecies Communal Cemetery 8
Langdorp Churchyard 61
Laud, Doris 60
Laud, Ronald 60
Lay, Philip 69
Laytmer School 29
Le Cateau 8
Le Culot 12
Le Havre 30, 34, 109
Lech 10
Leeuwarden 20
Leigh, Thomas 89
Leipzig 71, 73
Leitrim 99
Lemvig Cemetery 17
Lent, Helmut 20, 52
Les Grand Chapelles 9
Leuven 92
Light Night Striking Force 102
Lightholler, Herbert 1
Lincoln 52
Lincoln Cathedral 31
Linton, Adam 101
Little Rollright 80
Little Sandhurst 85
Little, Martin 87
Liverpool 23, 44
Llavallol Cemetery 77
Lock, David 39
Lockwood, Hilda 36
Lomas de Zamora 77
London 4, 20, 29, 36, 59, 87, 89
Long Bennington (St. Swithun) Churchyard 54
Lorient 13, 66
Lossiemouth Burial Ground 16
Lough MacNean 99
Loughborough 50
Luther, Elspeth 58
Luther, Flora 58
Luther, Luke 58
Luther, Wallace 58
Lyon, William 1

Maastricht 8
MacFarlane, Donald 35
Macgregor, Horace 4
Machum, Donald 95
Machum, Ian 95
Machum, Mrs 95
Macintyre, D.E. 63
MacIntyre, Flight Lieutenant 81
Macintyre, John 63
MacKay, Eric 82
Magdalen College 9
Magdeburg 106
Maidstone 77
Mainwaring, Ranulph 30
Malherbe, François de 47
Maloney, Pilot Officer 104

Manchester (Philips Park) Cemetery 66
Manchester 66, 77
Margate 18
Marissel French National Cemetery 33
Marjoss Civil Cemetery 83
Marlow Cemetery 79
Martin, Jean 7
Martin, Sydney 7
Matthews, Charles 11
Maubeuge-Centre Cemetery 55
Maudslay, Henry xiii, xviii
McCartney, Paul 23
McColm, Harold 28
McCrae, John 15
McCreery, John 83
McDonald, Hannah 51
McDonald, Robert 51
McDonald, William ix, x, 51
McGuigan, William 95
McIndoe, Archibald 4
McKee, John 79
McKenzie, John 30
McLean, James 102
McLennan, Burns xviii
Medemblik General Cemetery 62
Medhurst, Joseph 29
Melton Mowbray 53
Middlesborough 5
Milan ix, 51
Miller, Bruce 54
Miller, Maud 36
Missing Research and Enquiry Service xv
Mitchell, Stanley 39
Mittelland Canal 102
Modane 71
Mönchengladbach 20, 44
Montluçon 72
Montreal 41
Mordaunt, Thomas 27
Morsalines 91
Moss, Des 108
Mülheim 62, 63
Mullingar 99
Munich 91
Murray, Dennis 12

Nagelhout, Jacob 52
Nanton 92
National Provincial Bank 23
Neepawa 81
Newton, Leslie 37
Nias, Pilot Officer 52
Nichol, L. 69
Nichols, Bert 80
Nichols, Frederick 80
Nichols, Netties 80
Nienburg 52
Noakes, Frederick 11
North Gosforth Joint Burial Ground 13
Northampton 77, 107
Norwich 36

122

Norwich Cemetery 36, 69
Nottingham 19
Novack, Eva 98
Novack, Nicholas 98
Novack, Philip 98

Oakland 52
Old Halves 2
Oldenburg 1
Oliver, Frederick xiii, xiv, xviii
Oliver, Kathleen xiii, xiv, xviii
Olivos 77
Oostende New Communal Cemetery 11
Orangeville Bottling Works 32
Ostend 11
Oxenham, John 28
Oxford (Botley) Cemetery 68, 77, 80
Oxford 58
Oxford University 76

Pack, Sergeant 40
Paris 57
Parow 25
Partington, John (senior) 47
Partington, John 47
Partington, René 47
Patterson, James 10
Pedley, Alan 28
Penarth Cemetery 16
Penrith 69
Peral Harbor 45
Pershore Cemetery 74
Peterhouse College 77
Phillips, Frank 101
Pihen-lès-Guînes Communal Cemetery 23
Pilborough, Gertrude 40
Pilborough, William (senior) 40
Pilborough, William 40
Pinn, Geoffrey 91
Plahte, Viktor 80
Plaxtol Churchyard 94
Pleasance, Madeleine 47
Ploner, Mariaberta 10
Ploner, Rupert 10
Plungar 54
Poissy 33
Port Elizabeth 99
Portesham 23
Postlethwaite, D. 69
Potter, Brian 36
Potter, Nova 36
Potter, Royal 36
Poznan Old Garrison Cemetery 89
Preston 50
Preston Capes 77
Princetown 47
Prinz Eugen 47
Punta Arenas 51
Putney Vale Cemetery 23

Queen Alexandra's Imperial Military Nursing Service 44

RAF Alconbury 37
RAF Binbrook 79
RAF Boscombe Down 51
RAF Cottesmore 53
RAF Downham Market 59, 102
RAF Driffield 27, 32
RAF East Moor 66
RAF Elsham Wolds 38, 78, 83
RAF Exeter 27
RAF Graveley 94, 101
RAF Grimsby 47, 54, 82
RAF Halton 89
RAF Hampstead Norris 69
RAF Hemswell 2
RAF Honeybourne 100
RAF Honington 18
RAF Jurby 4
RAF Kirmington xiii, 97
RAF Lakenheath 39
RAF Langar 54
RAF Leconfield 91
RAF Lindholme 20, 86
RAF Linton-on-Ouse 15, 40
RAF Lissett 58, 72, 106
RAF Lossiemouth 16
RAF Marham 13
RAF Methwold 107
RAF Middleton St. George 78
RAF Oakington 19
RAF Oulton 14, 17
RAF Pershore 74
RAF Pocklington 32, 41, 56
RAF Saltby 53
RAF Skellingthorpe 51
RAF Snaith 36
RAF Stradishall 34
RAF Stratford 74
RAF Swanton Morley 12
RAF Swinderby 42
RAF Upper Heyford 68, 77, 80
RAF Waddington 52, 99
RAF Wattisham 1
RAF Wellesbourne Mountford 66
RAF Wymeswold 50
RAF Wyton 8, 21
Ramsey Cemetery 21
Rance, Sarah 85
Rance, Sidney 85
Randers Statsskole 61
Randwick Intermediate High School 57
Ray, Rupert 75
Raymond, Ernest 75
Read, Aubrey xvi
Reagan, Ronald 78
Reichswald Forest War Cemetery xviii, 38, 39, 63, 64, 84, 94, 104, 107
Reindeer Lake 62
Remnant, James xv
Renner, Irvine 57
Reynolds, LAC 6

Rheinberg War Cemetery 29, 31, 34, 35, 41, 44, 46
Rhys, Ernest 76
Rice, Grantland 42, 104
Rice, James 103
Riches, Derek 41
Roach, Fred 92
Robb, Elizabeth 32
Robb, Reginald 32
Robb, Walter 32
Roberts, Eric 70
Roberts, Sergeant 83
Robertson, John 27
Robertson, Weston 33
Robson, Thomas 12
Rochdale Cemetery 69
Rogerson, Bruce 38
Rostock 25
Rotterdam (Crooswijk) General Cemetery 72
Rotterdam 72
Royal Engineers 47
Royal Norfolk Regiment 99
Roye-Amy 109
Runnymede 56, 59

Sadler, Irene 50
Sagan 89
Sage War Cemetery 1, 2
Saint-Cyr-l'École 97
Salisbury 44
Salisbury Hospital 51
Sandhurst (St. Michael) Churchyard 85
Saunders, Peter 33
Savard, Joseph 63
Saxby & Farmer 47
Sayers, Basil 33
Scharnhorst 82
Schendelbeke 92
Schnaufer, Heinz-Wolfgang 59, 61, 71, 91
Scholven-Buer 104
Schoonselhof Cemetery 91
Schot, J 37
Scone 57
Scott, Walter 27
Scott-Martin, Anthony 31
Scott-Martin, Edith 31
Scott-Martin, Paul 31
Seuss, Theodor 59
Shakespeare, William 91
Sheffield 21
Shelley, Percy Bysshe 102
Shoreham by Sea 62
Silverstone 68
Simonides 75
Singapore 99
Skegness 37
Smith, Edgar 28
Smooth, Ronald 21
Smyth, D.C. 24
Snaefell 4
Socx Churchyard xviii
Southy, Robert 84

123

Spender, Stephen 78, 102
Spofford, George 76
Sproxton 53
SS Ceramic 44
SS Maaskerk 54
St Francis of Assisi 37
St Johns (Newfoundland) 58
St Omer 23
St Paul's Cathedral 106
St Thomas (Swansea) 55
St Trond 12
St. Andrew's Presbyterian Church 77
St. John the Baptist Anglican Cathedral 77
St. Michael (Barbados) 54
St. Nazaire 38, 40
Stalag Luft I 89
Stalag Luft III 89
Stalag Luft VIII-B 43
Stapleford 22
Starbeck 101
Sterkrade 103
Stettin 25, 28
Stewart, John 106
Stockton, Norman 79
Stoke-on-Trent (Hanley) Cemetery 16
Stratford-on-Avon Cemetery 66
Streib, Werner 22
Stuttgart 70, 78, 99, 101
Summerhayes, Pilot Officer 92
Surbiton Cemetery 59
Sutton Valence School 77
Swales, Wing Commander xiii
Swansea 55
Sydney 42, 57
Sydney High School 57
Sylt 13

Tansley, Alice 102
Tansley, Fred 102
Tansley, Mervyn 102
Taylor, Emily 65
Taylor, Frederick 65
Taylor, Katherine 65
Taylor, Leslie 65
Templeton, Pat 45
Tennyson, Alfred 29, 46, 58, 79
Terlinchtun British Cemetery 5
Ternhill 15
Tetley, Arthur 44
Tetley, Ellen 44
Tetley, Moira 44
Tetley, Norman 44
Texel (Den Burg) Cemetery 24, 56
Texel 24, 56
The Air Forces Memorial 56, 59
The Green Park 4, 92
The London Gazette 55, 66, 85, 97, 99, 109
The Saint Andrew's Scots School 77
Tholen 37
Thomas, Howard 16

Thompson, Dennis 101
Thompson, Lily 101
Thucydides 4
Tinker, Betty 21
Tinker, James 21
Tod Lake 62
Tod, Richard 62
Tod, Robert 62
Tonder Cemetery 23
Toowong 97
Toowoomba 42
Toronto 32
Tottenham Cemetery 16
Tottenham, Anthony 99
Tottenham, Arthur 99
Tottenham, Harold 99
Tottenham, Nicholas 99
Tottenham, Veronica 99
Tracey, Charles 24
Tranent New Cemetery 102
Tredegar 13
Trincomalee War Cemetery 5
Trinity Hall 47
Troyes Cemetery 9
Truxler, Lieutenant 85
Tucker, Bertram 73
Tucker, Frederick 73
Tucker, Lilian 73
Turnbull, Geoffrey 83
Turnhout 91
Tyler, William 35
Tyler, William 35

Unger, Sergeant 98
University of Sydney 57, 91
Urmston 77

Vancouver 67
Vancouver Island 98
Veendam General Cemetery 20
Veensloot 20
Velindre 55
Venlo 57
Venlo Military Cemetery 57
Vennes, Joseph 74
Versailles 97
Vivian, Edward 20
Vlieland General Cemetery 56, 65
Vrist 17

Walker Isabella 53
Walker, Anne 53
Walker, Doreen 53
Walker, Irene 53
Walker, John 53
Walker, Raymond 53
Walker, Thomas (junior) 53
Walker, Thomas 53
Wallis, Barnes 50
Walrond, Arthur 54
Waltham 82
Waltrop Municipal Cemetery 38
Warnemünde 25

Waterloo 52
Watson, Donald 30
Watson, George 30
Watson, Marquerite 30
Watts, Joyce 67
Weller, Alice 16
Weller, Cecil 16
Weller, Joseph 16
Wellingborough School 23
Wellington 45
West Bridgford 19
West Hampstead 20
Westbury-on-Trym ix, 2
Westernhope Moor 69
Westgate 69
Weymouth 23
Whittlebury 68
Wigan xiii, 100
Wilde, Alan 100
Wilde, Emily 100
Wilhelmshaven 1, 2
William, Ralph 24
Williams, Alfred 55
Williams, Bernard 107
Williams, Charles 2
Williams, Charles ix
Williams, Eliseus 105
Williams, Elizabeth 55
Williams, George 107
Williams, Graham 55
Williams, Rose 107
Willmer, Bernard 27
Wilsele Churchyard 90
Wilson, Jack 57
Wimille 5
Winchmore Hill 8
Winnipeg 81
Wintzenbach Protestant Churchyard 101
Wissant 99
Wissant Communal Cemetery 99
Witham 9
Wonseradeel (Makkum) Protestant Cemetery 43
Wood, Frank 17
Wood, Thomas 25
Woodhouse Eaves 50
Woodman, J.H. 67
Woods, Sergeant 53
Wren, Christopher 106
Wunstorf 105
Wuppertal 58, 59
Wyn, Goronwy 105

Yapham 32
Yeulett, George 106
York 36, 66

Zeebrugge 18, 47

PER ARDUA AD ASTRA
AN AIRMAN
OF THE
1939-1945
WAR
ROYAL AIR FORCE
29TH JANUARY 1944
KNOWN UNTO GOD